The Volcanic Eruptions of

El Malpais

A Guide to the Volcanic History and Formations of El Malpais National Monument

Marilyne V. Mabery
and
Richard B. Moore and Kenneth A. Hon
of the U.S. Geological Survey

*Prepared in cooperation with
the National Park Service Staff
El Malpais National Monument*

ANCIENT CITY PRESS
Santa Fe, New Mexico

For information address: Ancient City Press, P.O. Box 5401
Santa Fe, New Mexico 87502
Telephone (505) 982-8195

Cover illustration: Steve Tongier
Cover design: Kathleen Sparkes, White Hart Design, Albuquerque
Book design: Kathleen Sparkes, White Hart Design, Albuquerque

Mabery, Marilyne V.
    The volcanic eruptions of El Malpais : volcanic history and formations of El Malpais National Monument / by Marilyne V. Mabery : researched by Richard B. Moore and Kenneth A. Hon.
        p. cm.
    Includes bibliographical references.
    ISBN 0-58096-007-3 (pbk. : alk. paper)
    1. Geology—New Mexico—El Malpais National Monument.
    2. Volcanism—New Mexico—El Malpais National Monument.
    3. El Malpais National Monument (N.M.) I. Moore, Richard B. II. Hon, Kennneth A. III. Title
QE144.E5M33 1999
551.21'09789'91—dc21   98-51880
                                                        CIP

10   9   8   7   6   5   4   3   2   1

FOR YOUR SAFETY

Most trails in El Malpais National Monument and surrounding areas are rugged and unimproved. The trail guides provided in this book are suggestions, not precise maps. If you hike, be sure to carry plenty of water and wear a hat as well as sturdy hiking boots. It is hot in the summer, and most of the trails consist of uneven lava. Moreover, it is advisable to use safety gear such as hard hats, protective clothing, gloves, and flashlights when entering lava tubes. Do not shine lights on or disturb any animals in caves or in the open. A high-clearance vehicle is necessary for backcountry roads in the remote sections of the monument. However, do not travel these roads during rainstorms or other times when roads are wet.

Be sure to consult with the rangers concerning exact directions to the areas you wish to visit and about current road and weather conditions. Never hike alone, and always let someone know where you are going and when you expect to return.

For more information, call:
The National Park Service
El Malpais Information Center
(505) 783-4774

CONTENTS

PREFACE

The volcanoes of El Malpais silently hold the stories of their spectacular past. We have attempted to unravel parts of these stories by comparing the volcanic features of El Malpais to deposits we have watched form during active eruptions in Hawaii. Though we have brought some new perspectives to the volcanic history of the El Malpais region, much of the hard work necessary to understand such volcanic activity was done by other scientists. For the past two decades, A. W. "Bill" Laughlin and his associates have devoted a great deal of time and energy to solving questions related to the age and source of the lava flows. Charles Maxwell made the geologic map of El Malpais and determined the physical relationships between lava flows. Tracey Cascadden used chemistry and magnetic properties to further refine the relationship of lava flows from Lava Crater, Twin Craters, Cerro Candelaria, Lost Woman Crater, and El Calderon. In addition, ongoing research is led by Bruce Rogers, Cindy Mosch, Mike Goar, and many others who have contributed greatly to mapping and describing the cave systems.

The purpose of this guidebook is to help park visitors understand and locate the features preserved within El Malpais National Monument (National Park Service) and the surrounding El Malpais National Conservation Area (Bureau of Land Management) situated outside the city of Grants, New Mexico, south of Interstate 40. A glossary is provided as an aid to comprehending the geologic terms; and diagrams, photographs, and maps are included to assist readers in visualizing the volcanic history of the monument and identifying present-day features. Information about sites and their accessibility was provided by the National Park Service (NPS) and Bureau of Land Management (BLM) visitor centers.

El Malpais National Monument and El Malpais National Conservation Area were created to preserve and protect the unique volcanic land forms within the 590-square-mile boundary. Many of these features are extremely fragile, especially caves and cinder cones, and can never be repaired if damaged. Please be sure to check with National Park Service personnel for information on current road conditions and access to specific features described in this book before setting out to explore this isolated area. Inclement weather can make roads impassable, and other conditions can alter accessibility to certain features at any time.

The Ranger Station (BLM) on New Mexico 117 and the Information Center (NPS) on New Mexico 53 are open daily from 8:30 to 4:30 year-round. Both centers, which are 15 miles south of town, show videos illustrating the rugged nature of the landscape and hazards that exist. Some of the cinder cones and lava tubes around Bandera Crater are owned by the Candelaria family and are not within the national monument. Visitors to Bandera Crater and Bandera Ice Cave are charged a fee. Access to Cerro Bandera, Lava Crater, and Cerro Candelaria requires permission of the Candelaria family and is generally granted only for research purposes. Collecting rocks, plants, wood, or anything else is not allowed either within El Malpais National Monument or on the Candelaria property without permission.

Ranger tours are available during the summer; check at either center for times and locations. It is best to visit the park only during daylight hours. If you intend to explore this rugged area on your own, it is prudent to have a hiking partner in case of trouble. The importance of being prepared is stressed to all visitors by the monument staff: wear sturdy shoes, take along food and water, come expecting to encounter this challenging landscape on its own terms, and your visit will be unforgettable.

The sense of surprise that comes from stumbling upon the hidden wonders of El Malpais lends a unique feeling of discovery not experienced in starker, more barren volcanic fields like those of

Craters of the Moon National Monument in Idaho and Lava Beds National Monument in California. This is because forests of ponderosa pines, piñons, and junipers that have grown from minimal soil and bare rock blanket the area with deceptive greenery. Cave entrances, collapse pits, and even cinder cones often remain hidden in the trees until they suddenly appear out of nowhere at the last moment. Despite the sense of wonder this fosters, it is all too easy to wander deep into the forest only to be surrounded by a myriad of tortured lava forms that offer no clear way back. While a map and compass are more useful than bread crumbs, there is no substitute for keeping a keen eye out for the few rock cairns and landmarks that exist. It is wise to be aware of the isolated primitive nature of El Malpais and arrive prepared in order to enjoy this unique area.

ACKNOWLEDGMENTS

We owe a debt of gratitude to the National Park Service staff, particularly Ken Mabery, chief ranger, who not only provided background and logistical support but also acted as technical editor and caption layout editor for the manuscript. We are also grateful to Leslie De Long, chief of Visitor Services, who provided interpretative material for the text. In addition, the Candelaria family very graciously allowed us access to their land. Finally, many thanks to everyone else who helped us.

Getting Around in El Malpais

E ven today, few roads cross the broken surface of El Malpais. Visitors traveling by car are limited to skirting its north, east, and west edges along New Mexico Highways 53 and 117. Although vast expanses of lava flows can be seen all along New Mexico 117, few of the most spectacular volcanic features of the monument are visible from the highway. While it is possible to reach El Calderon cinder cone and Bandera Crater from short side roads off New Mexico 53, exploring other cinder cones, lava tubes, and flows requires a willingness to travel on unpredictable dirt roads and hike sometimes obscure trails. Information concerning trail and road conditions can be obtained at the New Mexico Visitor Center on Interstate 40, at the BLM Ranger Station on New Mexico 117, or at the Information Center on New Mexico 53. These centers also sell U.S. Geological Survey topographic maps and offer free park brochures and maps that give information about the places described in this book.

1

THE LANDSCAPE OF EL MALPAIS

CYCLES OF BIRTH AND DEATH

Long before the first human footstep fell on North America, volcanic eruptions repeatedly rocked the area around El Malpais, cracking the ground open, spraying lava skyward, and filling the air with pungent gases. Great outpourings of lava torched the land with intense heat and paved the countryside with hard, black rock. A few weeks or years after awakening, each volcano died nearly as suddenly as it had come to life. Then uneasy silence fell across the land, which could last for thousands or tens of thousands of years before the ground shook again to herald the birth of yet another volcano.

Gradually, life clawed its way back onto the hardened landscape and began reclaiming it. The process was slow and arduous, as can be seen by the twisted forms of trees scattered today across the youngest flows in El Malpais. Trees that sprouted in cracks jammed their roots deeper and deeper into the hardened lava, eventually breaking the surface into smaller and smaller pieces. Winds whipping off the desert drove tiny sand grains across the lava flows, building a fledgling soil that turned the tide in favor of life (Figure 1).

Figure 1. *Ancient ancestral Pueblo gate on the McCartys flow. The largest trees are ponderosa pines, growing in cracks where windblown dust traps water. Photograph courtesy of U.S. Geological Survey personnel.*

By the time the first Native Americans set eyes on this land, the cycle had been repeated nearly a hundred times during the previous million years. The oldest of these volcanoes was long dead, and its lava flows were covered by soil, with only the smoothed forms of cinder cones and volcanic craters betraying the violent past of the region. The younger and more rugged flows and craters of El Malpais appeared then much the same as today; eons of rain and snow have done little to change the surface of the earth here.

To survive here meant it was necessary to remain connected with the land, and over time the Pueblo people learned to adapt to the harsh landscape. The volcanic craters and flows of the landscape left an indelible impression on the earliest inhabitants of this region, who incorporated these geological features into their oral traditions. Thus, the prehistoric Pueblo people and their descendants, the Acoma and Zuñi people of today and the Navajos who arrived later, not only survived in these surroundings but revered them. Tales of lava flows soon became intertwined with their creation stories and other narratives elucidating their religions and lifeways within this high-desert landscape. All of the Native American cultures of the region incorporated the prominent landscape features into their traditions and named most of the volcanic flows and peaks. Although many of the native names of local topographical features have been replaced by Spanish and Anglo designations for general usage today, the Pueblo and Navajo residents still refer to the cones and flows by their traditional names among themselves.

One example of the many oral traditions associated with the area is the Acoma Pueblo epic of a ruthless gambling Kachina and his twin sons, who blinded him so he would not destroy their people. Black lava blood flowed from the Kachina's eyes, ruining all that lay in its path. As it cooled, it solidified into serpentine ropes and cresting waves of black rock, producing ice caves where water could be found year-round for the Acoma tribe and their animals.

Another example of an oral tradition associated with the region is the Navajo legend of twin war gods who slew monsters to protect the human race. The El Malpais country affirms the mythological history of the Navajos, for it provides concrete evidence of the congealed blood of these monsters in its lava flows, confirming that the war gods did slay the monsters to protect their people. Here the twin war gods—Born for the Water and his brother, Monster Slayer—consulted their father, the Sun, and Changing Woman, their mother, about how they could help the Navajo people and received advice as well as holy arrows and other devices to assist them in destroying the monsters. After many battles in which the twins were almost killed, they finally subdued their most powerful enemies and recognized that the remaining monsters should be left alone so that the world would not become overpopulated and misused.

Not only were the lava flows and their mysterious caves important Indian religious sites, they also provided water, ice, and game for individuals journeying between pueblos. With the arrival of the Spanish conquistadors, El Malpais offered protection and hideouts for native people who knew its secrets. However, for the Spanish this rugged sea of rock was merely a barrier more treacherous than any ocean. The jagged rocks and vast expanses of lava could be life-threatening to men traveling on horseback who were encumbered by heavy armor and ignorant of its hidden dangers. Because this desolate land seemed so menacing to the Spanish, as a warning to future travelers, they marked it on their maps as El Malpais, "the bad country."

However, the remote and intimidating nature of El Malpais that caused the Spanish to fear it is perhaps its greatest attraction now. Isolation has kept the land in a nearly pristine state. Hidden within the boundaries of El Malpais National Monument and the conservation area are some of the most beautiful cinder cones, lava flows, and lava tube caves found in the United States. The extensive volcanic activity of the area is impressive, with thirty-three major volcanic vents, and fifteen distinct lava flows within the monument's boundaries. The volcanic activity at El Malpais has given researchers and visitors alike life-long opportunities to explore and be mystified by its endless variety. Every volcanic event here heralded a new landscape and new challenges to the high-desert environment. Approximately every 7,000 to 25,000 years over the last 100,000 years a new lava landscape appeared following an eruption. First primitive soil began to form on the lava surface, then plants slowly covered the new lava flows. Thus this rugged land chronicles both ecological and geological events that date back millions of years. While the importance of all this is just beginning to come to light, the lesson to be learned about the power of volcanic activity is evident everywhere. The story of the volcanic eruptions at El Malpais lies locked within the hardened lava.

ZUÑI-BANDERA VOLCANIC FIELD

Approximately 2.5 to 3.5 million years ago lava poured out of the earth, spreading across portions of western New Mexico, which may not have been as rugged as the present-day landscape of the region.

Figure 2. *Mount Taylor, an eroded stratovolcano, in the distance. In the foreground are landslide blocks from the old, lava-capped mesa near Grants that forms the horizontal ridge in the left center of the photograph. Photograph courtesy of U.S. Geological Survey personnel.*

Rock from deep within the earth began to melt and rise into weakened zones of the crust. Then molten rock, called magma, worked its way upwards until it erupted at the surface as lava flows. Most of the lava was very fluid and spread out to form the black flows that now cap most of the colorful mesas east of the monument and east of New Mexico 117, such as Mesa Negro and Cebollitta Mesa (Plate 1). Also during this period eruption of stickier lava piled up to form Mount Taylor (Figure 2), the prominent stratovolcano seen to the north of El Malpais and Grants. Mount Pagan seen erupting (Plate 2) in the Northern Mariana Islands is an example of a stratovolcano.

The Mount Taylor volcanic field and the later Zuñi-Bandera volcanic field in the monument are only two of the major volcanic fields aligned along a great zone of weakness that extends from northeastern New Mexico to eastern Arizona called the Jemez volcanic zone

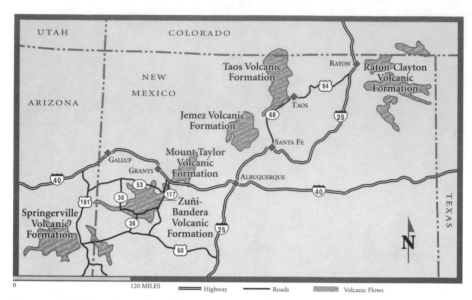

Figure 3. *Map of northern New Mexico and part of Arizona showing the location of major volcanic fields.*

(Figure 3). It includes the volcanoes around Capulin Volcano National Monument, the Jemez Mountains and Valle Grande Caldera near or north of Bandelier National Monument, the Mount Taylor volcanic field, the Zuñi-Bandera volcanic field, and the Springerville volcanic zone of east-central Arizona.

The forces tearing at the Colorado Plateau were produced as California was dragged against the Pacific Continental Plate for hundreds of miles along the San Andreas fault. This sliding motion, coupled with the opening of the Gulf of California during the past 5 million years, caused most of the western United States to be stretched to one and a half times its original size. This stretching not only pulled the Colorado Plateau west, it pushed the plateau upward as hot, plastic rock from the mantle rose beneath this enormous block of continental crust.

Rivers that had meandered gently across the originally flat surface began to cut deeply into the surrounding rock as it rose, producing canyons and goosenecks etched into the stone. The Rio Grande now occupies a deep valley, called a rift, produced by the tearing away of the Colorado Plateau. Canyons were carved all over the Colorado Plateau, slicing through lava and layers of multicolored sandstone, shale, and limestone that were laid down by oceans, wind, and streams over the past 50 to 500 million years. Where the canyons cut deepest or where the sedimentary layers were thin, such as in the Zuñi Mountains, just north of El Malpais, granites and 3- to 4-billion-year-old metamorphic rock were exposed.

The valleys cut around El Malpais are relatively broad and wide compared to the spectacular chasms of Canyonlands, Bryce, Zion, and the Grand Canyon, which were also formed during this time. The majestic San Francisco Peaks, volcanoes south of the Grand Canyon, are scenic testimonials to the close relationship between canyons and other volcanic features on the Colorado Plateau.

2

EL MALPAIS ERUPTIONS

Most of the eruptions at El Malpais began in the following way: Tremors, at first barely perceptible, gradually strengthened as molten rock forced its way to the surface, cracking apart solid rock on its way. Soon everything shook noticeably, the result of hundreds of earthquakes so close in succession that they felt like one continuous event. Finally, the earth split open, and lava flew into the air. The cracks spread quickly as if the ground were being unzipped. Lava erupted over the entire length of the fissures, forming "curtains of fire" hundreds of feet high (Plate 3). Within hours or a few days, parts of the fissure cooled and solidified, forcing the lava out of fewer and fewer openings. Since the amount of lava erupting remained relatively unchanged, its confinement to fewer vents greatly increased the pressure and caused it to shoot even higher, creating "fire fountains" that sprayed lava more than a 1,000 feet into the air (Plate 4).

In most volcanic fields, fissures tend to follow specific directions (Plate 5). At El Malpais all of the vents are aligned roughly southwest to northeast. When examined closely, fissures are not single straight cracks but systems of smaller segments that show a consistent offset to one side or another. Although little of the original fissure systems remain at El Malpais since most have been buried during later stages of eruption, the alignment of vent structures shows that the original fissures were at least ¼ to 1 mile long, with individual segments a few hundred yards in length.

ASCENT OF LAVA

In geological transformations of this nature, deep beneath the earth's crust heat is generated by great tectonic forces and begins to melt the surrounding rock. Temperatures are in excess of 2,500°F, while pressures are more than 10,000 times that of the atmosphere at sea level. Thin films of melted rock form along the edges of tiny mineral grains, like sweat on your skin. The melt does not drip because it is hotter and lighter than the surrounding rock. It flows together, forming a large buoyant mass that rises gently like a hot-air balloon launched through cooler air.

The amount of carbon dioxide (one of the gases we breathe in low concentrations in the air) contained within the melt has a big influence on how fast the mass of molten rock rises to the surface. Under such great pressure, the carbon dioxide in the melt is so compressed that it is either liquid or completely dissolved in the melt. The more carbon dioxide in the molten rock, the lighter it is and the faster it rises. As the molten rock or magma approaches the surface, bubbles of carbon dioxide begin to form and expand, driving it even faster.

At El Malpais the journey of molten rock began 30 to 50 miles below the earth's crust. Some of the magmas rose so fast they ripped pieces of solid rock from deep within the earth's mantle and carried them all the way to the surface. At Bandera Crater ("flag" in Spanish) and some of the older cones in El Malpais, there is evidence that the lava rose and erupted fast enough to eject pieces of the mantle. These fragments are called xenoliths, meaning "foreign rocks" in Greek (Plate 6). Two types of xenoliths are found in the Bandera flows: a dark green type that may be related to formation of the lava, and a light green type that is not related to the lava. The largest xenolith found in the Bandera lava is more than 1 foot in diameter. To carry such large pieces of mantle, the molten rock that fed Bandera eruptions must have ascended at 1 to 5 miles per hour. The entire trip of approximately 50 miles from where it melted to the surface may have taken as little as 10 hours—an astonishing rate considering it had to travel through solid rock!

COMPOSITION OF LAVA

All of the lava erupted at El Malpais is the black type called basalt. Basalt lava is made up of about half silica (the material that window glass is made of) and half elements like aluminum, magnesium, iron, and calcium. High iron content and magnesium make this lava look black. Basalt lava is so fluid that expanding gases, primarily steam, can bubble out of it during an eruption. Because of this fluidity, most basalt eruptions are not very explosive.

Two varieties of basalt are found at El Malpais. One type that is rich in the alkali elements of potassium (K) and sodium (Na) is called alkali basalt. This variety is common on many ocean islands. The other type has a very low alkali content, especially in potassium, and is called tholeiitic basalt (pronounced thow-lee-itic, a name taken from a small island off Great Britain). Tholeiitic basalts, the most common rocks on the earth, make up most of the mid-ocean ridge volcanoes and oceanic crust. Ninety-five percent of tholeiitic basalts are under water. By contrast, alkali-rich basalts tend to have more carbon dioxide, and probably more water, resulting in much more spectacular eruptions and higher cones.

Lavas with more silica, such as the dacites of Mount St. Helens (about ⅔ window glass) and the rhyolites of Mount Taylor and Yellowstone (about ¾ window glass), are more viscous, or sticker, than basalt. Expanding bubbles cannot easily escape such lava and eventually blow it into tiny pieces of volcanic ash. Thus, eruptions of rhyolite and dacite lava tend to be very violent when they contain water. Rhyolite and dacite lava form thick masses that pile up like toothpaste around vents.

FUEL FOR ERUPTIONS

Ordinary steam, like that which whistles from a teapot, is the major force behind most volcanic eruptions. When held at great pressure underground, water remains dissolved within the magma, similar to the manner in which a soda can or bottle holds carbon dioxide gas. When the ground cracks and the pressure is released, the steam can expand 100 to 1,000 times its volume, propelling the lava high into the air. Shaking up a can of soda and opening it produces a very similar effect, though at a much lower temperature.

The amount of water and carbon dioxide within the lavas at El Malpais seems to have been directly related to whether they are the high-potassium or low-potassium variety. The high-potassium alkalic basalts had lots of water and carbon dioxide that caused them to shoot high into the air, while the low-potassium tholeiite basalts had much less gas and flowed more gently out of the ground.

3

VOLCANIC
FORMATIONS

T he volcanic cones in El Malpais National Monument have grown in several different ways, beginning from only a crack in the ground. In this area the shape of the cone is directly related to the type of lava that produced it, although this is not always the case in other volcanic regions.

CINDER AND SPATTER CONES

During volcanic eruptions gas-rich alkalic basalts yielded foamy lava then shot it high into the air as fire fountains, named for the red-hot droplets of lava they spray (Plate 4). These fire fountains spray lava in much the same way as a fire hose sprays droplets of water straight up into the air. Fire fountains may either be continuous or consist of many closely spaced explosive bursts.

Small pieces of bubbly lava spewed from the fire fountains and, cooling as they fell, piled up to form cones of loose particles called cinders. Continuous fire fountains produce a thick pile of cinders, while explosive bursts make many thin layers of cinders and fling out very

Figure 4A and 4B. *Bombs on El Calderon. Photographs courtesy of U.S. Geological Survey personnel.*

dense fragments called bombs (Figures 4A and 4B). Cinder cones produced by the eruption of alkali basalt are easily identified by their conical shape and central depressions, called craters. Examples of cinder cones found at El Malpais are El Calderon, Lost Woman Crater, Twin Craters, Bandera Crater, Cerro Candelaria, Cerro Bandera, and Paxton Crater (Figure 5).

By contrast, gas-poor, low-potassium tholeiitic basalts generated very low fire fountains no higher than 100 to 200 feet, if any at all. Instead of being foamy, lava was flung as Jell-O-like blobs called spatter (Plate 7). Spatter is formed by low fire fountains and small bursts caused by shallow degassing of lava. Such fire fountains more closely resemble water coming from a garden hose with the nozzle held vertically, producing a small column. In low fire fountains, the lava does not break into a spray of finer droplets as it does in high-pressure fire fountains. This continuous outpouring of fluid lava built very low, smooth vents called lava shields or shield volcanoes (so named because they look like a warrior's shield). These volcanoes are not easily identified by most people as lava vents. At El Malpais, examples of shield volcanoes produced by the eruption of tholeiitic basalt are the McCartys Crater, Cerro Hoya, Cerro Rendija, Lava Crater, and the north side of El Calderon (Figure 5).

SPATTER, CINDER, ASH, AND BOMBS

Lava thrown from volcanoes takes on a variety of shapes depending on the energy of the eruption and the stickiness of the lava. The lowest-energy eruptions fling large blobs of lava called spatter (Plates 7 and 8). If the spatter is relatively cool when it lands, the individual blobs are preserved. Most spatter ranges from a few inches to 1 foot long and has a smooth surface. Narrow, twisted forms are called ribbon spatter, while larger, flat blobs are called cowpie spatter. At El Malpais, most spatter has a shape between these two types, with ribbon spatter being fairly rare.

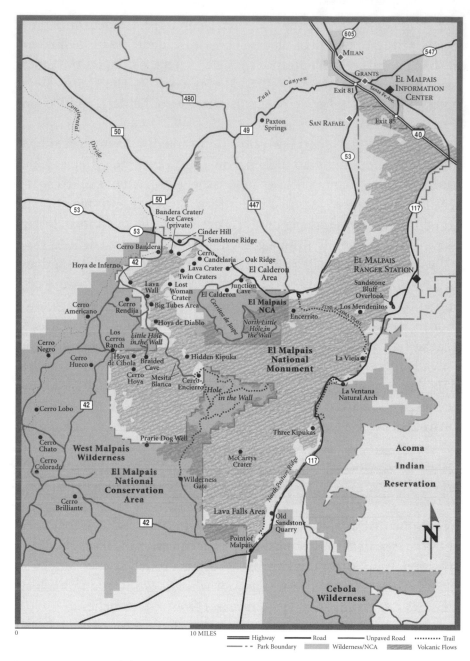

Figure 5. *Map of the El Malpais National Monument area showing the locations of some features discussed in the text.*

Figure 6. *Massive layers of agglutinate on the north flank of Bandera Crater on the inner rim, showing partly welded spatter, with the individual fragments still visible. Layers on the inner north flank of Bandera Crater completely welded spatter with no trace of the original pyroclastic structure. Photograph courtesy of U.S. Geological Survey personnel.*

Almost all spatter is still plastic when it hits the ground and shows evidence of deforming, or "splatting." If the spatter is only slightly molten when it lands, it will weld together, a type of spatter common at the summit of Cerro Rendija and found locally at Bandera Crater (Figure 6), Lost Woman Crater, and Cerro Candelaria. Spatter that is still liquid when it lands can move downhill like a lava flow and is called agglutinate. The rim of Lava Crater is made up entirely of agglutinated spatter that has frozen in drip-like formations. Spatter that sprayed out of the crater to the east fed two lava flows that flowed around the western side of Cerro Candelaria.

Cinders are cooled droplets of lava foam that vary in size from about ¼ inch to 2 inches in diameter (Plate 9). Cinders are generally very light and distinguished from spatter by their smaller size and their bubbly texture that looks like frozen foam. In contrast to the smooth surfaces of spatter, bubble holes show on most cinder edges. Dense cinders have small bubbles like foam rubber, while light cinders have big bubbles like foamy soap. Some cinders are partly covered by a very thin glassy veneer that indicates they were still molten when they fell. Good examples of these cinders can be found in the cinder pit on El Calderon (Plate 10).

If cinders are still partly or completely molten when they fall back to the ground, they can form welded deposits, or agglutinates, just like spatter. In fact, it is very common for cinders falling from the outer part of a continuous fire fountain to cool and fall to the ground, while those in the center stay very hot and fall back as liquid to feed large lava flows. Fire fountains fed by explosive bursts tend to be cooler and produce more cinders, resulting in much faster cone building.

The smallest cinders and tiny sand-sized particles called volcanic ash are generally carried to the highest part of the fire fountain by rapidly rising hot air. From the top of the column, these fine particles can drift several miles downwind before covering the landscape. Good examples of downwind deposits of black cinders and ash can be seen along New Mexico 53 just east of Bandera Crater on the north side of the highway.

Strong explosive bursts not only produce cinder and spatter but can eject extremely heavy, dense fragments of lava called bombs, which range in size from less than 1 inch to over 3 feet in diameter. Most bombs have very few bubbles and show evidence of being rolled up in layers. Such layers form when lava lands on a steep slope and rolls back downhill like a wet snowball. Some bombs have dense foreign rock fragments in their cores, like green mantle xenoliths. Many bombs are aerodynamically shaped as they fall, partly molten, through the air (see Figures 4A and 4B). Large bombs more than 1 foot in diameter often make impact craters where they fall in cinders. However, such craters are easily destroyed by other natural or artificial processes, and are therefore rarely preserved for long.

Bombs commonly have long tails when falling, but these are very brittle and break off upon landing. Bombs that were partly molten when they fell, and thus had long tails and aerodynamic bodies, are called spindle bombs. Good examples of these can be seen at El Calderon. Other bombs, called accretionary bombs, are nearly spherical and were solidified before they were blown out of the crater.

Because bombs are so heavy, they tend to fall very close to a crater rim. While they can be thrown farther, most found away from the cone have bounced down the sides and rolled to their present positions. For example, the bombs littering the eastern side of Bandera Crater rolled and bounced off the cone.

CONE FORM AND COLOR

Cones are often described as breached, meaning that their symmetry has been broken by a lava flow that interrupts the smooth continuity of the crater rim (Plate 11). The image that the word *breach* conjures up is one of an already-formed, perfectly circular cone that suddenly is torn apart by ascending, laterally spreading lava flow that carries away part of the cone's flank. In reality, cinder and spatter cones almost invariably are breached from their beginning. This is because lava flows typically start welling upward, moving downslope, and spreading laterally at almost the same time as the beginning of the vertical, gas-rich, jetting phases of the eruption that produce cinders and spatter. Flowing lava "rafts" may carry away parts of the cone, especially if the amount of lava being erupted suddenly increases. When such blocks of cone material cool and are examined more closely, they can be easily recognized, and may be found miles from any other vent material. For example, a section of Bandara Crater's rim was rafted to the Lava Wall area about 5 miles from the crater.

Cinder or spatter cones often form during only a single eruption; some cones, however, such as the currently active Pu'u O'o on Kilauea Volcano in Hawaii, may erupt several times over the course of years. At El Malpais, the great size of the cones, the large volume of associated flows, and the absence of any significant soil horizons between flows from the same vent show that these eruptions occurred only once. The term monogenetic is used to describe cinder cones and associated flows that formed during a single eruption (Plate 12). Most cinder cone volcanoes worldwide are monogenetic; however, a given volcanic field may have hundreds of monogenetic vents that erupted over an extended period of time.

Cinder cones can attain heights of 1,500 feet or more above their bases. The highest cone in the vicinity of El Malpais is probably 700-foot-high Cerro Brillante in the National Conservation Area, off County Road 42 near the southwestern edge of the monument. Cinder cones are usually higher than spatter cones, partly because spatter cools more slowly, tends to become welded, and may flow a short distance away from the vent. Many, if not most, large cinder cones also contain significant amounts of spatter, reflecting temporary changes in the amount of gas dissolved in the lava. Often a cone composed mostly of cinders will have an "armor" of spatter on its surface, showing the decrease in gas of an eruption near its end. Such protective spatter armor dramatically slows the usual erosion of cinders from cones.

To casual observers, spatter cones do not appear much different from cinder cones, but as noted above, spatter cones tend to be smaller and lower, although there are many exceptions. In addition, spatter cones are often elongated, since they are commonly built up along lengthy eruptive fissures (Plate 13), whereas cinder cones tend to be nearly circular since they are often built at a single vent or group of closely spaced vents.

Cinder and spatter cones display a striking profusion of colors, including red, black, brown, and pale yellow. On some of the cones small patches of black stand in stark contrast to red hues. These strong color variations do not reflect differences in the types of eruptions but rather the way lava fragments cooled after landing. The color differences basically reflect whether the iron in the basaltic cinders is in the ferrous ($Fe+O_2$, unoxidized) or ferric ($Fe+O_3$, oxidized) state. If water is around, either from the lava itself or from rain that often accompanies eruptions, the hot cinders react with it, and the iron is converted from the black ferrous state, the color at the time of eruption, to the oxidized, red ferric state. Sometimes the presence of a buried tree or other organic material can cause the iron in cinders to be converted back to the ferrous state from the ferric state. Brown color is transitional between original black and oxidized red and often means that the cinders are quite old and weathered. Yellow and other colors usually indicate staining by sulfur or secondary minerals that formed in steamy fumaroles as the cinders cooled. At El Malpais, the best and most colorful cinders can be found on Cerro Americano.

SHIELD VOLCANOES AND LAVA LAKES

Shield volcanoes, so named because they resemble a warrior's shield lying on its back, are built up almost entirely by lava flows, with little or no spatter or cinders. The resulting shape is quite flat compared to cinder or spatter cones. At El Malpais, examples are Cerro Hoya, Cerro Rendija, Lava Crater, and the McCartys vent. Shield volcanoes are common features in volcanic fields around the world. The Hawaiian Islands consist of large shield volcanoes built up from the Pacific Ocean floor over hundreds of thousands to millions of years (Plate 14).

In Hawaii, during historic time (approximately the past 200 years) eyewitnesses have described eruptions that built three lava shields superimposed on the larger shield of Kilauea Volcano. They are some-times called satellite shields, because they are constructed on the surface of a much larger shield volcano. Mauna Iki formed Kilauea's southwest rift zone during 1919 to 1920; Mauna Ulu formed on Kilauea's upper east rift zone during 1969 to 1974; and recently, Kupaianaha erupted on the middle east rift zone from 1986 to 1992, producing flows that destroyed about 180 homes and the village of Kalapana. Kilauea lava shields are comparable in size to Cerro Rendija and the other shield volcanoes in El Malpais National Monument.

At Kupaianaha, the top of the shield, which had partly collapsed, held a crater in which a lava lake, filled by magma slowly welling up from below, continuously circulated for six years. This lake drained southeastward through a tube that insulated the lava from cooling and enabled it to retain its fluidity 8 miles or more downslope to Kalapana. At Mauna Ulu, surface lava was temporarily dammed, forming a "perched," shallow lava lake on the flank of Mauna Ulu, which eventually drained away through a tube. A similar perched lava lake may be seen near Bat Cave in El Malpais National Monument. Perched lava lakes generally are smaller and shallower than lakes associated directly with a volcanic vent.

4

LAVA RIVERS

W hen fluid lava is erupted, it is either flung into the air by gas-rich explosions that build a cinder or spatter cone, or it flows on the ground (Plate 15) or into a body of water. Lava flows, although hotter, denser, and more easily subject to freezing than water, behave in much the same way as most other liquids. Lava seeks the lowest points on the earth's surface, often flowing through valleys eroded by streams, such as Zuñi Canyon (Figure 5). The speed of lava is so great it can actually flow uphill if it is blocked from going any farther in the direction it has been moving, although this situation is fairly rare.

PAHOEHOE AND `A`A LAVA

Lava usually flows away from its vent as either pahoehoe (pronounced pa-hoy-hoy) or `a`a (pronounced ah-ah), both Hawaiian words. Pahoehoe is smooth, often ropy lava (Plates 16 and 17), while `a`a is the rough, loose type (Plate 18). Pahoehoe lava can change into the `a`a type, especially when it cascades over a cliff, loses coherence, and becomes desegregated. However, `a`a lava can never change into the pahoehoe variety, because the temperature necessary to cause remelting does not occur at the earth's surface.

It may be difficult to understand how a rough-surfaced `a`a flow can move at all. The reason is that under the visible surface is a liquid core of lava, often many feet thick, propelling the flow downslope. Sometimes a crack will develop in the flow's upper surface, and the molten core will gush out, forming a patch of slightly younger pahoehoe in a sea of `a`a—a phenomenon that could give the false impression that the `a`a lava changed into the pahoehoe type.

CHANNELIZED AND SHEET `A`A

The mass of moving rubble called an `a`a lava flow tends to build levees along its margins or between active and stagnant flow lobes. Levees form because the edge of the flow cools quickly and stops moving, whereas the hotter center of the flow moves faster, leaving the cooled rubble behind. Levees confine the flow to a relatively narrow channel, depending on the size of the eruption and volume of lava being extruded over a short period of time. An increase in the amount of lava feeding the flow can overtop or push aside the marginal levees, causing the flow to widen.

If the volume of lava being extruded is very large over a short period of time (some eruptions have exceeded 500,000 cubic yards per hour), and if the slope being covered by lava is quite steep, then `a`a lava may not form levees but instead rush downslope as a non-channelized sheet flow (Plate 19). Outstanding examples occur on the steep slopes of Mauna Loa and Hualalai Volcanoes on the Island of Hawaii. At El Malpais, the land surface is generally too flat to allow extensive development of `a`a sheet flows. Most of the `a`a lava at El Malpais is in the flows from Bandera Crater, and most of that appears to have formed relatively late in the eruption, after the tube-fed pahoehoe flows. Exposures of Bandera Crater `a`a along the Zuñi-Acoma Trail include sheet flows.

SHELLY PAHOEHOE

Shelly pahoehoe is what the name implies, pahoehoe so thin, light, and full of gas holes (vesicles) that it breaks like a shell when stepped on. Shelly pahoehoe is one of the more dangerous types of lava, especially when it has just formed. If you are unfortunate enough to step on shelly lava during an active eruption and fall through the crust into molten lava or a hot tube below, you will have a serious problem, if you survive at all. At El Malpais, however, where the most recent eruption occurred about 3,000 years ago, no such problem exists now.

Shelly pahoehoe typically forms near the edges of pahoehoe lava channels, as a result of repeated overflows caused by temporary increases in the amount of lava entering a channel. Small, short, thin flows surge over the tops of channel walls and move a few feet downslope, cooling and freezing quickly. Shelly pahoehoe is most commonly found near channels that are close to their source vent, because sudden changes in flow volumes are more pronounced there. Farther from the vent, changes tend to be more modulated because of the greater distance from the cause of the change. Shelly pahoehoe is also common on flows near their source vents, or next to low spatter ramparts. Here, the pahoehoe is thin, most of it having flowed much farther away, and full of vesicles, since it froze before the gas could escape (Plate 20).

At El Malpais, some of the best exposures of shelly pahoehoe can be found near lava channels on the east side of El Calderon, and around the collapsed pit crater about 1 mile north of Cerro Hoya, near Lava Crater, and along the Big Tube Trail (Figure 5).

PAHOEHOE SHEET FLOWS

Pahoehoe flows that advance without benefit of lava channels or heat-conserving lava tubes are called sheet flows. They characteristically have smooth upper surfaces with little relief (change in elevation). Typically, they form on preexisting gentle surfaces, in contrast to `a`a sheet flows. Good examples of pahoehoe sheet flows can be seen while hiking over the McCartys flow in the Lava Falls area or from the Sandstone Bluffs overlook.

TUBE-FED PAHOEHOE

Tube-fed pahoehoe is lava that flowed through tubes (Plate 15) rather than having been emplaced as a sheet flow. Being insulated from cooling on all sides, tube-fed flows lose very little heat (in Hawaii sometimes only 2° over 10 miles). Thus, they can advance many miles, depending on the duration of the eruption and the slope of the preexisting ground surface. Tube-fed pahoehoe flows at El Malpais include those from Cerro Rendija, Cerro Hoya, El Calderon, Lava Crater, and Bandera Crater. These flows can be seen off New Mexico 53 (Figure 5). Tube-fed pahoehoe is a precise geologic term with no `a`a equivalent.

SLAB PAHOEHOE

Slab pahoehoe is a type of lava flow that is transitional between smooth, ropy pahoehoe and `a`a. It can form in at least three ways: when the top crust on a pahoehoe flow fails due to a lack of support from below; by lateral pressure when one flow lobe runs into another, making a solid lobe; or by lava cascading over a small cliff. At El Malpais good examples of slab pahoehoe can be seen on the Lava Crater flow near El Calderon or at the Lava Falls area off New Mexico 117 (Figure 5).

HUMMOCKY PAHOEHOE

Pahoehoe is often hummocky, the result of what is usually called lava blisters and tumuli. Lava blisters are small, rarely more than 3 feet across, and form when gas in the flow expands and bows up the pahoehoe surface. A tumulus is generally larger than a blister, as wide as 100 feet, and forms on gentle slopes when the flow's advance is obstructed and lava beneath the surface bows up the crust of the flow. At El Malpais, good examples occur on the McCartys and El Calderon pahoehoe flows (Figure 5).

5

LAVA TUBES AND INCANDESCENT CAVES

F ew experiences in life are as startling as the first view of a skylight, an opening into an active lava tube (Plate 21). During an
eruption, desolate expanses of black lava appear very solid until
you come across one of these windows into the glowing red world
that lies below. The nearly invisible heat rising from a skylight can hit
you like a blast furnace and singe your eyebrows right off if you are
not paying attention. And beneath what seemed like solid rock lies a
river of molten lava in an incandescent cave reminiscent of Dante's
Inferno. The surface paths of active lava tubes are commonly only
perceptible to the trained eye, and as little as 1 foot of lava is all that
may separate you from the fiery realm below.

FORMATION OF LAVA TUBES

Early workers envisioned lava tubes as passageways completely filled
with lava that gradually drained as the eruption feeding them
waned. Their notion was that lava flows were emplaced as thick
masses of liquid lava and that internal shearing of the fluid lava

resulted in the formation of lava tubes. However, observations of active lava flows in Hawaii have led to quite a different view of tube formation. We now know that most thick lava flows are constructional; that is, they are built up either by successive flows or by an internal increase in lava that raises the upper surface, or roof, of the lava flow. At El Malpais, a walk out to the Big Tubes area (see page 52) will make it evident that you are climbing up a constructional feature to reach the lava tubes.

Lava tubes, like those that created the Big Tubes and related caves, are formed when lava channels roof over. Since lava is very fluid, like water it tends to follow the lowest areas as it flows over the ground. Lava flows will follow gullies if they are present, but gullies are not necessary for the formation of lava tubes.

Lava channels form both in `a`a and pahoehoe flows by the piling of cooler, slower-moving material to the sides of the lava flows. If the eruption lasts long enough, a quenched crust begins to form on the surface of a lava channel, and eventually the channel becomes completely roofed over. Over time, the crust continues to grow in from the sides of the channel and in the downstream direction. Very small lava channels can crust over in a matter of hours, while larger ones may take days or even weeks. The formation of a lava tube system in large channels requires a delicate interplay between the amount of lava erupted, the speed of the flow, and the duration of the eruption.

RED-HOT EROSION

The initial shape of a lava stream is much like that of a river, relatively wide in comparison to its depth (Figure 7). Lava tubes that we have observed forming are typically 3 to 6 feet deep and 10 to 30 feet wide at first. Soon after roofing over, the crust continues to cool and thicken over the roof of the lava channel, decreasing the amount of space available for the lava to flow. Pressure builds up within the newly formed tube and generally results in outbreaks of pahoehoe lava along

Steeply Sloping Ground

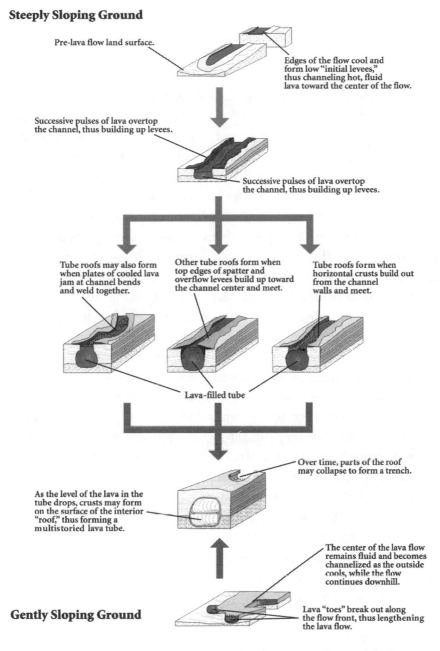

Pre-lava flow land surface.

Edges of the flow cool and form low "initial levees," thus channeling hot, fluid lava toward the center of the flow.

Successive pulses of lava overtop the channel, thus building up levees.

Successive pulses of lava overtop the channel, thus building up levees.

Tube roofs may also form when plates of cooled lava jam at channel bends and weld together.

Other tube roofs form when top edges of spatter and overflow levees build up toward the channel center and meet.

Tube roofs form when horizontal crusts build out from the channel walls and meet.

Lava-filled tube

Over time, parts of the roof may collapse to form a trench.

As the level of the lava in the tube drops, crusts may form on the surface of the interior "roof," thus forming a multistoried lava tube.

The center of the lava flow remains fluid and becomes channelized as the outside cools, while the flow continues downhill.

Gently Sloping Ground

Lava "toes" break out along the flow front, thus lengthening the lava flow.

Figure 7. *Development of lava tubes. Drawing by Bruce Rogers, U.S. Geological Survey. From* Natural History of El Malpais National Monument.

the crest of the tube system. These outbreaks serve to rapidly thicken the roof of the tube and increase the insulation of the lava below.

The early stages of tube construction are determined by the interaction between hot lava and a very cold environment encountered when a flow erupts. The erupted lava flow crosses cold ground and is surrounded by air that sucks the heat away, causing a large portion of the lava to "freeze," forming a crust. As a tube forms and is covered with insulating lava flows, a much greater amount of heat from new lava passing through it is trapped within the tube walls. This heat is conducted by contact with the walls and causes the least crystallized parts of the surrounding floor and walls to begin melting again.

Lava is nearly three times as dense as water and exerts a tremendous force on anything over which it flows—just ask anyone who has stuck something in a lava stream and tried to retrieve it. When the underlying lava begins to get mushy from remelting, the lava stream can begin to erode into it. This causes the tube to gradually deepen, leaving a space between the lava river and the roof of the tube. The shape of the tube naturally progresses from a sideways oval, to a roughly circular form, and finally to the upright oval shape common to most large lava tube systems. The final form of a tube is related to eruption duration, lava supply, and slope. Although the width of a tube system changes very little, tubes commonly end up about ten times deeper than the lava stream that created them. Thus, it is unlikely that the 30- to 80-foot-deep lava tubes of the Bandera system ever had more than 6 to 10 feet of lava flowing within them. Most of the big bends in tube systems reflect curves formed by the original lava channels, although the down-cutting processes can produce smaller side passages (Plate 22). Large rooms and side passages are primarily the result of temporary downstream blockages that resulted in the outbreak of new flows with new tube systems. These rooms may also be formed when eroding tubes cut into older systems and reoccupy them.

Lava in its molten state is 2,500° F. Heat radiating from a channel, much like very intense sunlight, keeps the walls and roof of the tube at temperatures only slightly cooler (50° to 212°F) than the lava itself but still hot enough to remelt about 25% to 50% of the rock. Without the lava stream to support the walls, the remelted liquid in the walls and roof oozes through pore spaces similar to the way water moves through the holes in a kitchen sponge. This gravity-driven melt forms droplets of remelted lava that eventually "sweat" off the walls and roof to form small "soda straw" stalactites and droplet structures that coat the walls and floors of many tubes.

As the melt extrudes from the walls, it is exposed to high concentrations of oxygen in a lava tube, immediately bonding to iron in the rock. This reaction produces iron oxide minerals (similar to magnetite) that bind with other crystals in the melt to form a skin that holds these delicate features together. Sometimes extreme melting of the walls results in slumping of this skin into folded "elephant skin" texture (see the egg-shaped feature, plate 27). In addition, there is a wide variety of other textures and shapes in tubes resulting from this combination of crystallization, melting, and erosion.

When an eruption finally ends, most of the fluid lava drains from the tube system, leaving a more viscous "sludge" of lava slowly moving down the tubes. These dregs of the lava system are what we see after cooling as the ropy, spiny, and clinkery lava on the floors of most tubes that are not covered by collapse rubble. At El Malpais, the best example is the floor of Four Windows Cave.

After an eruption, the tubes slowly cool, and the iron minerals tend to oxidize (or rust, like scrap iron) into the smooth red-brown coatings found on many of the original lava tube surfaces. Although these coatings have the appearance of very solid rock, broken pieces reveal that they are only .07974 of an inch thick with many irregular cavities. This zone of melting is typically only about 8 to 12 inches thick in most lava tubes. Beyond this zone, the rock making up the walls of the tubes appears more like typical lava flows seen on the surface.

Because lava tubes are constructional, they tend to be found very close to the present-day surface. Lava tubes that are more deeply buried tend to collapse and are nearly impossible to access. Thus, the origin of lava tubes contrasts markedly with the formation of lime-stone caves, which are created by the passage of water through rocks deep underground.

6

Dating the
El Malpais
Eruptions

etermining the ages of young volcanic rocks can be either
very simple or very difficult. Unfortunately, the latter has
turned out to be the case at El Malpais. Although geologist A.
W. Laughlin has persistently researched the ages of El Malpais lava
flows over the course of his career, despite the arsenal of high-tech
equipment at his disposal, lava flows at El Malpais have yielded only
a few reliable dates. Still, these are of great importance for understanding how the volcanic field formed. Laughlin used a total of six
methods to determine ages of the flows. Where multiple methods
were applied to the same flow, agreement between methods was
excellent. These methods included the potassium-argon (K-Ar)
method; the argon 40 method; the carbon 14 (C_{14}) method; the heli-
um 3 (He_3) method; the chlorine 36 (C10H6Cl8 36) method; and
the uranium series disequilibrium (U series) method.

The simplest method of determining age is relative dating.
Determining the relative age or sequence of eruptions is easy if lava
flows touch each other—the flow on top is the younger one.
However, many flows at El Malpais do not overlap and must be dated
in other ways. Even where flows do not touch each other, geologists

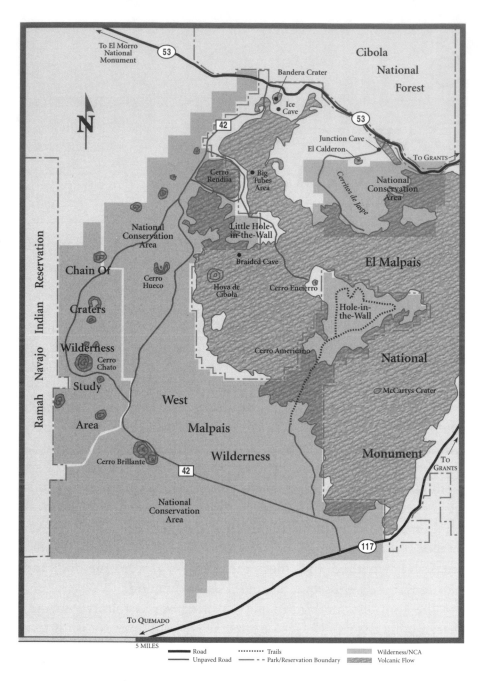

Figure 8. *Map of Chain of Craters Backcountry Byway.*

FOR YOUR SAFETY

Please be aware that County Road 42 is a type II byway that requires a high-clearance vehicle. The road is not paved, although its dirt and gravel surface is routinely graded by the county. It can be negotiated with a two-wheel-drive, high-clearance vehicle without undue difficulty. **However, wet weather conditions can make this road treacherous and impassable. Check with a ranger before you attempt to drive it.** Do not travel alone. Carry plenty of water, and if you hike be sure to wear a hat and sturdy hiking boots.

Because the Chain of Craters is remote, outstanding recreational opportunities abound. Although few established hiking trails exist, there are plenty of places to hike. Overnight camping is allowed in both El Malpais National Conservation Area and El Malpais National Monument. Vehicles are restricted to existing dirt roads, except in wilderness areas, where vehicles and mechanized equipment, including mountain bikes, are prohibited.

DIRECTIONS

The Chain of Craters Byway is located in Cibola County, near Grants. From Interstate 40, it can be accessed from New Mexico Highways 117 or 53. To begin the byway from the south entrance, turn south onto New Mexico 117 from Interstate 40, about 5 miles east of Grants; County Road 42 begins approximately 35 miles from the New Mexico 117 turnoff. To begin the byway from the north, travel Interstate 40 through Grants and take the San Rafael exit south. Travel on New Mexico 53 about 25 miles. County Road 42 begins on the south side of New Mexico 53.

can use several field techniques to distinguish between different lava flows and their relative ages, including abundance and size of the most common mineral phenocrysts that characterize basalt, amount of soil on top of the flows, degradation of original primary surface features, and color.

In addition to these methods, Laughlin used several other techniques to determine more precise ages of lava flows at El Malpais.

These dating techniques rely on analyzing radioactive decay of various elements, the two most useful being carbon (C) and argon (Ar). A limitation of the carbon method is that it can only date organic material less than 40,000 to 60,000 years old and requires finding the remains of dead plants beneath a lava flow. This can be very difficult in a desert environment with little vegetation. Although the argon method uses samples from the lava itself, a drawback of this method for dating volcanic features at El Malpais is that it frequently yields ages that are too old for rocks as young as those in this region. For a more detailed description of these dating techniques, read *Natural History of El Malpais National Monument* compiled by Ken Mabery (see Bibliography).

AGES OF EL MALPAIS ERUPTIONS

The rugged lava flows of El Malpais are the youngest part of the much larger Zuñi-Bandera volcanic field. Three distinct episodes of volcanism have been identified within the monument. All of these are younger than the mesa-forming flows that underlie East Grants Ridge and Cebollita Mesa.

The first eruptions in the Zuñi-Bandera field occurred between 500,000 and 750,000 years ago, corresponding to what A.W. Laughlin and others refer to as "Pulse 1" in *Field-trip Guide to the Geochronology of El Malpais National Monument and the Zuñi-Bandera Volcano Field, New Mexico*. These old lava flows are found in the far western and southern parts of the region (Figure 5). In most cases, their source vents cannot be found, either because erosion stripped them away, or more likely, because they have been buried by younger volcanic rocks. One of the more prominent examples of these early basalts is the 60-mile-long Fence Lake flow southwest of the monument. For location and access information, refer to park maps.

The second period of intense eruptive activity in the Zuñi-Bandera field occurred about 100,000 to 200,000 years ago, corresponding to

AGES AND TYPES OF LAVA FLOWS FROM EL MALPAIS

Lava Flows of El Malpais National Monument

Name	Vent	Type of flow	Age
McCartys	McCartys shield	pahoehoe sheet flows	3,000 years old
Bandera	Bandera Crater	`a`a and tube-fed pahoehoe	11,000 years old
Cerro Hoya	Cerro Hoya shield	pahoehoe sheet flows	Possibly younger than the Lava Crater flows
Lava Crater	Lava Crater shield	tube-fed pahoehoe	16,000 years old
Lost Woman Crater	Lost Woman cinder cone	channelized and tube-fed pahoehoe	Younger than Twin Craters flows
Twin Craters	Twin Craters cinder cone	channelized `a`a and tube-fed pahoehoe	Older than the Lava Crater flow
Candelaria	Cerro Candelaria	`a`a	Older than Lava Crater flows
El Calderon	El Calderon cinder cone and shield	`a`a flows followed by pahoehoe eruptions	115,000 years old

Lava Flows of the Zuñi Mountains North of El Malpais National Monument

Name	Vent	Type of flow	Age
Zuñi Canyon	Paxton Springs cinder cone	channelized `a`a	Younger than El Calderon flows
Oso Ridge	Oso Ridge cinder cone	`a`a canyon flow	Older than Zuñi, younger than El Calderon

Older Lava Flows from the Chain of Craters within El Malpais National Monument

Name	Vent	Type of flow
Plagioclase lava	South Rendija shield	pahoehoe sheet
Cerro Rendija	Cerro Rendija shield	shelly and tube-fed pahoehoe
Cerro Encierro	Cerro Encierro shield	tube-fed pahoehoe

"Pulse 2," of Laughlin and others. Cones and flows that erupted during this time are not eroded much, although they are commonly partly buried by windblown dust. The cones in the Chain of Craters and their flows (west side of County Road 42) erupted during this time (Figures 5 and 8). Notable examples from this period are Cerro Arizona, dated at about 150,000 years, and El Calderon, approximately 115,000 years old. Cerro Arizona is located in the northern Chain of Craters, about 5 miles south of New Mexico 53 via County Road 42. El Calderon is about 3 miles southeast of the monument's Information Center off New Mexico 53.

The third period of young volcanism in the El Malpais area, what Laughlin and others refer to as "Pulse 3," apparently began about 16,000 years ago with the closely spaced eruptions of Cerro Candelaria, Twin Craters, Lost Woman Crater, and Lava Crater. Cerro Hoya and the three vents and associated flows in the Zuñi Mountains may have erupted at around the same time. The McCartys cone and flow are much younger than the others (about 3,000 years) and can be taken as an indication that volcanic activity may not have ended in the Zuñi-Bandera volcanic field.

7

Exploring the Volcanic Features of El Malpais

E l Malpais National Monument includes the products of at least fifteen separate volcanic eruptions, which formed eleven cinder cones, four shield volcanoes, and at least fifteen distinct lava flows. The above number of flows is a minimum; most basaltic eruptions result in several separate flows that go in different directions. Usually, but not always, the flows are formed from a single eruptive event and have similar chemical compositions and phenocryst populations. It is also likely that several lava flows are buried beneath younger deposits. All of the youngest eruptions were apparently long-lived, for they resulted in large cinder cones or shield volcanoes at their vents, as well as extensive lava flows that commonly extended for several miles.

We will describe these features in reverse chronological sequence, beginning with the youngest, and listing the Keresan (Acoma) and Navajo names for each volcano where known (in some cases the names are no longer part of the cultural memory of our Native American informants). El Malpais is a natural wonder open to the public, and a premier area where resource preservation is paramount. Please do not remove any samples since their value can only be assessed if they remain where they are found.

McCARTYS CRATER AND FLOW
Kau pa ta Kh bä yanish (Keresan)
Navajo name unknown

The McCartys flow, named for the small town near its distal end along Interstate 40, is one of the largest and most voluminous young basalt flows in the southwestern United States. In 1993, A. W. Laughlin and others radiocarbon-dated it at about 3,200 years B.P. The total length of the flow is about 36 miles, and its volume is at least 2 cubic miles. However, the estimated volume is dependent on uncertain variable thickness, and could differ from the above figure by perhaps ± 30% to 40%. This high volume, the gentle surface gradient on the preexisting rocks, and the predominance of pahoehoe all suggest that the McCartys eruption probably lasted for several years.

The McCartys flow is mostly black, glassy, relatively smooth pahoehoe, but it includes patches of rougher `a`a and slab pahoehoe. In many parts of the flow, high-standing pahoehoe surrounds small crater-like features that R. L. Nichols called collapse depressions in his 1946 article "McCartys Basalt Flow, Valencia County, New Mexico." However, more recent work by Ken Hon and others reported in "Emplacement and Inflation of Pahoehoe Sheet Flows: Observations and Measurements of Active Lava Flows on Kilauea Volcano, Hawaii" has shown that these features are not the result of collapse. Instead, they are inflated pahoehoe that has surrounded but not quite covered a formerly high area on the pre-lava surface or a lava surface from an earlier episode of the same eruption (see Plates 23A and 23B).

Hornitoes (Figure 9), small spatter cones built over a crack on an active lava flow, are common in a few areas of the McCartys flow. Typically, they formed where inflated pahoehoe sheets developed cracks that extended deep enough to tap the still-molten lava beneath the solidified surface. The lighter, less dense molten lava rose through the cracks and "erupted" spatter and small flows for a short time, building cones (Figure 10).

Figure 9. *Hornito on the McCartys flow. Note the bulbous masses of partly welded spatter. Photograph courtesy of U.S. Geological Survey personnel.*

Figure 10. *Large hornito on a flow from Bandera Crater near the Candelaria Ice Cave. Photograph courtesy of U.S. Geological Survey personnel.*

Figure 11. *Small cinder cone (darkest low hill in the center of the photograph) atop the shield volcano at the vent for the McCartys flow. Note the `a`a flow in the foreground. Photograph courtesy of U.S. Geological Survey personnel.*

A small cinder cone (Figure 11), about 25 feet high, atop a low shield volcano marks the vent for the McCartys flow. Apparently, gas-rich cinders were ejected near the end of the eruption, although the amount of gas more commonly decreases through time during most eruptions that have been witnessed elsewhere in the world. Perhaps a new magma source was tapped near the end of the eruption. This suggestion is in accord with J. R. Carden and A. W. Laughlin's observation in *Petrochemical Variations within the McCartys Basalt Flow, Valencia County, New Mexico* that plagioclase, a felspar mineral, is the most abundant phenocryst near the vent, whereas olivine is more abundant farther away.

Next to New Mexico 117, in the southeastern part of El Malpais National Monument, is the Lava Falls Trail (Figure 5), which crosses 2.5 miles of the McCartys flow. The trail provides access to excellent examples of primary surface features, such as ropy lava, inflation ridges with large cracks, and inflation depressions, on a fresh, young pahoehoe flow. Some of the primary features are illustrated in Figure 12, photos A, B, C, D.

Figure 12. *Primary, uneroded surface features on the McCartys flow. (A) shows a tumulus, where lava pressure from below formed a dome on the surface of the lava flow. (B) shows pahoehoe toes that crept over the older flow from Cerro Hoya. (C) shows a large crack in the McCartys sheet flow; in some places, this crack was deep enough to tap still-molten lava below the thick crust, and hornitoes formed next to the crack. (D) shows a ridge that is an inflated flow front. Photograph courtesy of U.S. Geological Survey personnel.*

In addition, vegetation on the flow illustrates the complex interplay of surface cracks of variable sizes that trap and hold water, as well as the tenacity of plants in this desert climate. One of the more notable aspects of vegetation on the McCartys flow is that it appears quite dense with bushes, including lush cholla and prickly pear cactus, yet lacks the taller ponderosa pine of the neighboring older flows. The water demands of the larger trees must be much greater than those of the smaller plants on the McCartys flow, and necessary root systems for larger trees can be developed only on the older, soil-cov-

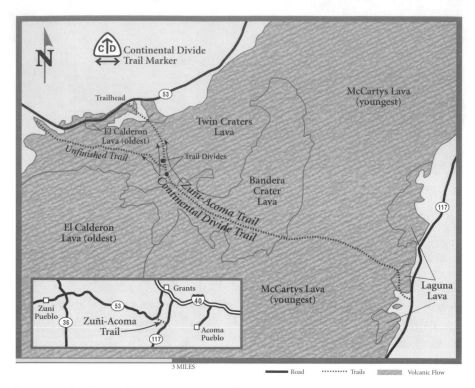

Figure 13. *Map of Zuñi-Acoma Trail.*

ered substrate. Geologic examination shows that much of the "soil" actually was blown in by the wind; and small dunes are common, especially on pre-McCartys rocks.

The rugged Zuñi-Acoma Trail (Figure 13) winds across about 3 miles of the McCartys flow and also traverses about 5 miles of older flows from Bandera Crater, the Twin Craters group of vents, Cerro Hoya, and El Calderon (Figure 5). People who hike the Zuñi-Acoma Trail can readily see the striking contrast in vegetation between the older `a`a and the younger McCartys pahoehoe. This trail is not recommended for people who are out of shape. Because of its difficulty, make sure you have the latest information on conditions and be prepared for strenuous hiking conditions.

FOR YOUR SAFETY

This is a rugged trail primarily consisting of uneven lava. It is 7 miles across and takes about 6 to 7 hours to hike oneway. Carry plenty of water, and wear a hat and good hiking boots. It is hot, and the lava stores heat. **DO NOT HIKE THIS TRAIL ALONE.** It is marked with rock cairns, but they can be hard to see. You may have to stand at one cairn while your partner looks for the next one. Many of the rock cairns were built long before Europeans arrived and have not been changed. Please do not disturb artifacts or the pristine terrain. Always check with a ranger before hiking this trail or any backcountry trails.

THE TRAIL

On the west side of the monument, the Zuñi-Acoma Trail begins on New Mexico 53, 16 miles south of Interstate 40. On the east side of the monument, the trail begins from New Mexico 117, 15 miles south of Interstate 40.

As you begin hiking the trail from New Mexico 53, you see the earliest lava flow in the valley, which came from El Calderon, the cinder cone 4 miles west. This flow underlies most of the other lava on the trail. Soon the lava flow from Twin Craters, which is 7 miles northwest of Bandera Crater, begins, a later lava flow with less plant life and weathering. In the middle of this flow is a limestone "island" the Acoma people call Encerrito, meaning surrounded. About 2½ miles from the trailhead you cross onto even younger lava, the flow from Bandera Crater. This flow has the most extensive lava tubes in El Malpais. About a mile further is the youngest lava flow in the valley, the McCartys flow, which started about 8 miles southwest at McCartys Crater and flowed north. Only 700 to 1,000 years old, it has many sinkholes and minimal vegetation. Just before you reach New Mexico 117, you cross down onto the older, underlying Laguna flow, which erupted from the volcano Hoya de Cibola, about 14 miles west of this area.

Figure 14. *Aerial view looking west of Bandera Crater and its blanket of black cinders. Photograph courtesy of U.S. Geological Survey personnel.*

BANDERA CRATER AND LAVA FLOW

Tsa me sh'tima (Keresan)
Dibė hogan (Navajo)

The second-youngest cinder cone and associated flows in and near El Malpais National Monument is Bandera Crater next to New Mexico 53, in the northwestern part of the volcanic field (Figure 14). Cinders from Bandera Crater were radiocarbon-dated in 1993 at about 11,000 years B.P. by A. W. Laughlin and others.

Bandera Crater (privately owned) is a large cinder-and-spatter cone approximately 800 feet high and ⅝ mile in diameter. The floor of the crater is about 260 feet below the preeruptive surface. Although commonly associated with late-stage explosive eruptions believed to enlarge craters, such a deep feature is usually a normal consequence of a fountain bottom. At that level, the gases (carbon dioxide, water vapor, hydrogen sulfide, and sulfur dioxide) that drive the eruptions are explosively ejected from the ascending magma as it suddenly encounters lower pressure near the earth's surface.

Flows from Bandera Crater are chiefly tube-fed pahoehoe and late-stage `a`a that extends as far as 22 miles from the vent. The origin of these flows is the break in the cinder cone's south wall. The estimated volume of all products of the eruption is at least 1.7 cubic miles, a figure that is highly dependent on uncertain flow thickness. By analogy with recent activity in Hawaii and elsewhere, eruptions at Bandera Crater probably continued for several years, perhaps with some relatively short pauses.

Lava flows and late-stage cinders from Bandera Crater contain xenoliths that originated in the earth's mantle. These samples, sometimes larger than 1 foot across, are found chiefly in the cinder pits on the north side of New Mexico 53, as well as scattered throughout the flow. Most of the xenoliths fall in the general category of peridotite (Plate 6), meaning they consist mainly of olivine, with lesser amounts of pyroxene and spinel.

One of the most remarkable features of this flow is its lengthy, highly-developed system of lava tubes, which has been identified as the longest system of tubes on the North American Continent. At least 17 miles of tubes have been discovered and explored thus far. The following sections contain descriptions of some of the tubes and other nearby features most accessible to the public (Figure 5).

LAVA WALL

More than 100 feet high in places, the Lava Wall (Figures 8 and 15) is a spectacular example of an `a`a flow terminus; it is found off County Road 42, north of the Big Tubes area parking lot. Huge `a`a flows, fed from eruptions at Bandera Crater, stopped when they hit the gentle northern slopes of the much older Cerro Rendija shield. The higher, eastern half of the Lava Wall is the earliest lava flow from Bandera Crater and was fed by high fire fountains. Large pieces of the cone up to 50 feet high slid onto the flow surface and were "rafted" about 3 miles to their present positions. The younger, western `a`a flow over-

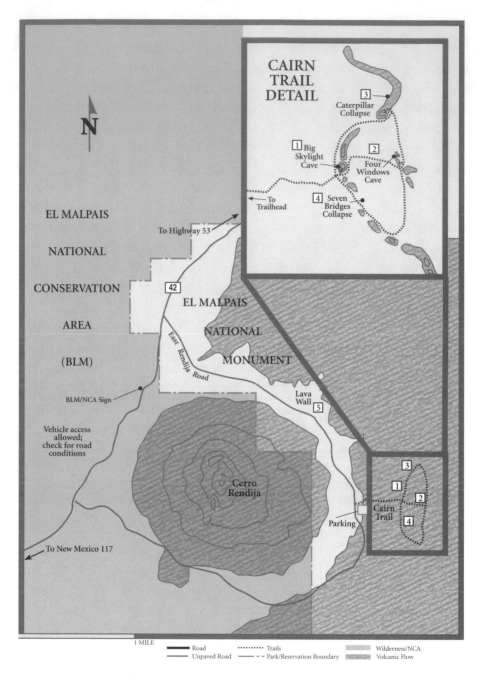

Figure 15. *Map of Big Tubes area.*

FOR YOUR SAFETY

A high-clearance or four-wheel-drive vehicle is needed to visit this remote section of the Bandera Lava Tubes system. **Travel in this area is discouraged when roads are wet. Be sure to check first with a ranger about road conditions.**

Help to protect the delicate moss beds by not walking on rocks covered with moss. Hard hats, boots, protective clothing, gloves, water, and three sources of light are necessary when entering lava tubes. **DO NOT HIKE ALONE.**

DIRECTIONS

To get to the Big Tubes area, drive 26 miles west on New Mexico 53 to County Road 42 south. There are two roads that allow access to the Big Tubes area parking lot. They are located 4.5 and 6.5 miles south of New Mexico 53. A cairn trail will lead you to Big Skylight Cave and Four Windows Cave.

laps the older flow where the Lava Wall changes direction from northwest to west. This flow is all spiny brown `a`a and lacks the large rafted blocks of a cinder cone.

LAVA TUBES

The most spectacular lava tubes at El Malpais (Figure 15) are from the youngest lava flows of Bandera Crater. The flows were fed by large rivers of lava confined by channels in rubbly `a`a flows. The surface of the channels crusted over, and the smoother pahoehoe lavas leaked out and covered much of the earlier `a`a. As the lava continued to flow through the tubes, the surrounding rock began to remelt due to the heat, and the lava river eroded downward and deepened the lava tubes to their present size (more than 90 feet in diameter in many places). The lava flowing through the tube system was probably never much more than 10 feet deep. A rugged ½-mile trail to the Big Tubes begins 3 miles east of County Road 42 (Figure 15). Follow the signs and check park maps for location. The following four features of the Bandera Lava Flow can be explored from this trail.

BIG SKYLIGHT CAVE

Big Skylight Cave (Figure 15) was an open, incandescent hole that overflowed with lava at least once while the flow was active. Now it provides light and rain for the fragile moss garden that grows beneath it. Please refrain from stepping on the moss since it is easily destroyed. The entrance to this cave lies at the south end of a large collapse trench. A natural bridge over this trench lies just a few yards north of the cave entrance.

Beautiful dripstone textures can be seen on the ceiling of the collapse and within the lava tube (Plate 24). These features formed as the ceiling and walls of the active tube heated up, remelted, and "sweated" lava. The prominent horizontal bands on the walls of the cave represent the level of lava as it gradually cut down and deepened the tube. Much of the roof of this cave has collapsed, leaving large piles of rubble on the floor. The hike through this cave is quite rugged since you must walk on the boulders from the ceiling collapse the entire length of the cave.

FOUR WINDOWS CAVE

After walking beneath the Four Windows (Plate 25) and past their moss-blanketed boulders, you drop onto the original floor of this lava tube (Figure 15). To the left of the main passage are two smaller lava tubes that formed by erosion at the floor level. The sculpted walls and high cathedral ceilings of the main passage are breathtaking, particularly if you can imagine them glowing orange from the

Plate 1. *Mesa Negro (center) and Cebollita Mesa (right), east of El Malpais National Monument, as seen from El Calderon cinder cone. Both mesas are capped by an erosion-resistant basaltic lava flow. Photograph courtesy of U.S. Geological Survey personnel.*

Plate 2. *Mount Pagan, an active stratovolcano in the northern Mariana Islands, erupting in April 1994. Fine brown ash is being ejected several hundred feet into the air and drifting eastward. Mount Pagan is a potentially dangerous volcano, and the people living on Pagan Island were evacuated during a major eruption in 1981. Photograph courtesy of U.S. Geological Survey personnel.*

Plate 3. *Curtain of fire on the first day of the eruption in April 1984 of Mauna Loa on the Island of Hawaii, the largest volcano in the world. The fire fountains are about 100 feet high. Photograph courtesy of U.S. Geological Survey personnel.*

Plate 4. *East rift zone eruption of Kilauea Volcano, Island of Hawaii, in March 1983. The fire fountain, as high as 800 feet, is inclined slightly to the east because of an obstruction in the vent. Photograph by Ken Mabery, National Park Service.*

Plate 5. *Fissure eruption of Kilauea Volcano, Hawaii, photographed in April 1982 in the summit caldera; note that the fissure is slightly curved. Photograph courtesy of U.S. Geological Survey personnel.*

Plate 6. *Light-colored xenoliths of peridotite from the earth's mantle in a basalt flow from Bandera Crater. Note that they are only slightly rounded, having been transported so rapidly from their source 25 or more miles below the earth's surface that only minor remelting occurred. Photograph courtesy of U.S. Geological Survey personnel.*

Plate 7. *Small, active spatter cone at Kilauea Volcano, Hawaii, during the April 1982 summit eruption. A large blob of spatter has just been expelled from the vent. Photograph courtesy of U.S. Geological Survey personnel.*

Plate 8. *Taken in January 1989 on the southeast coast of Kilauea Volcano, where spatter accumulated during brief fountaining after a lava bench collapsed into the ocean and exposed an open lava tube system. Photograph courtesy of U.S. Geological Survey personnel.*

Plate 9. *Eruption of Kilauea Volcano in April 1983, showing relatively cool, dark cinders falling from an incandescent eruption column that is about 400 to 500 feet high. Dust is rising where the cinders are pulverized after hitting the ground. Photograph courtesy of U.S. Geological Survey personnel.*

Plate 10. *Cinders from El Calderon. The larger fragments are bombs. Photograph by Ken Mabery, National Park Service.*

Plate 11. *Halemaumau Crater, within the summit caldera of Kilauea Volcano, Hawaii. Halemaumau, which is about _ of a mile in diameter, formed mostly during the twentieth century as a result of repeated withdrawal of magma from beneath it. Buildings on the caldera rim are a volcano observatory operated by the U.S. Geological Survey. Photograph courtesy of U.S. Geological Survey personnel.*

Plate 12. *Cinder cone in the process of formation on April 15, 1995, at the Fogo Volcano, Republic of Cape Verde. This cone eventually grew to be about 500 feet high. `A`a flowed to the left (north). Larger bombs litter the cinder field in the foreground. Photograph courtesy of U.S. Geological Survey personnel.*

Plate 13. *Spatter cones on Kilauea Volcano, Hawaii, a set of five or more low cones form as spatter is thrown a short distance through the air and flows out from the bases of the cones. Photograph courtesy of U.S. Geological Survey personnel.*

Plate 14. *Hawaii is home to the largest shield volcanoes on the earth, two of which are shown in this photograph from offshore Kona. The closer shield is Hualalai, which last erupted in 1800 to 1801; its ridge line appears bumpy because dozens of cinder cones erupted along its crest. In the background is Mauna Loa, the largest volcano in the world. The black flow in the foreground was erupted by Mauna Loa in 1859. Photograph courtesy of U.S. Geological Survey personnel.*

Plate 15. *Lava flow on the east rift zone of Kilauea Volcano in September 1977. The fire fountain at the source vent is in the distance. Note the large mass of rock from the lava channel walls being rafted down the flow. Photograph courtesy of U.S. Geological Survey personnel.*

Plate 16. *Large sheet pahoehoe flow in Hawaii. These houses in Kalapana were eventually destroyed by t he eruption of Kilauea Volcano, Hawaii. Photograph by Ken Mabery, National Park Service.*

Plate 17. *Active pahoehoe flow of the 1983 to 1997 (and continuing) eruption of Kilauea Volcano, Hawaii. The pahoehoe toe swelled until its thin, slightly cooled crust could no longer withstand the internal pressure of lava, and a new toe broke out. Photograph by Ken Mabery, National Park Service.*

Plate 18. *An active, incandescent, `a`a flow on Kilauea Volcano, Hawaii, in March 1983. Photograph courtesy of U.S. Geological Survey personnel.*

Plate 19. *A rough, cold `a`a flow from Bandera Crater. Photograph courtesy of U.S. Geological Survey personnel.*

Plate 20. *Holes and pits in rock called vesicles, which formed when gas bubbles were trapped in the lava flow. The flow continued to move after the vesicles formed, and thus they are somewhat stretched. Photograph courtesy of U.S. Geological Survey personnel.*

Plate 21. *Skylights (collapsed lava tube ceilings) allow views into active tubes in flows from Kilauea Volcano's continuing 1983 to 1997 east rift eruption. Note the remelted ceiling dripping into the tube. At El Malpais this feature is best seen at Big Skylight Cave. Photograph courtesy of U.S. Geological Survey personnel*

Plate 22. *Braided Cave, in a lava flow from Cerro Hoya; the main tube is to the left, and a smaller side tube disappears off to the right. Photograph courtesy of U.S. Geological Survey personnel.*

Plate 23A. *Inflation pahoehoe. sheet flows in Kalapana, southeast coast of Kilauea Volcano, Hawaii. Note the extraordinary thinness of the flow on the lawn. Eventually, these flows inflated and became much thicker.*

Plate 23B. *Inflation pahoehoe. Inflated sheet flow from McCartys Crater. The person is standing in a crater, about 60 feet deep, which formed when the younger lava flow thickened around a formerly high point on the pre-existing surface. Photographs courtesy of U.S. Geological Survey personnel.*

Plate 24. *Dripstone several inches long on lava tube walls in Big Skylight Cave. Photograph courtesy of U.S. Geological Survey personnel.*

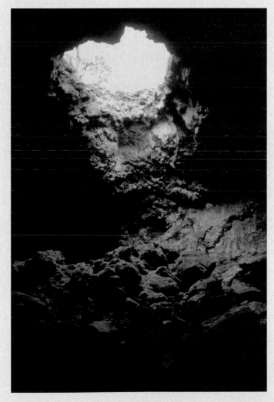

Plate 25. *Skylights in the ceiling of Four Windows Cave that gave the tube its name, with a garden of moss below the skylights. Photograph courtesy of U.S. Geological Survey personnel.*

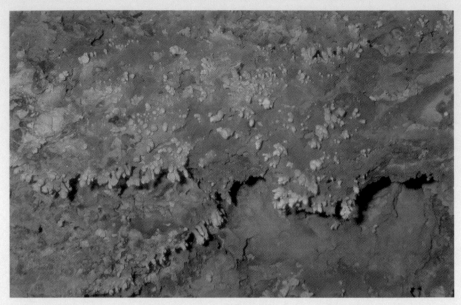

Plate 26. *Crusts of white secondary minerals on the walls of Four Windows Cave. Photograph courtesy of U.S. Geological Survey personnel.*

Plate 27. *Egg-shaped xenolith of sandstone, about 3 feet long, near the upper end of the tube that starts at a vent about 1/2 mile north of Cerro Hoya. The xenolith, which now has a frothy texture like pumice, was partly melted and smoothed by the basaltic lava flowing in the tube. Photograph by Ken Mabery, National Park Service.*

Plate 28. *Four cinder cones and their associated flows all formed at about the same time 16,000, years ago. 28(A) Cerro Candelaria from the southwest with Mount Taylor in the distance.*

28(B) Twin Craters looking northeast. Twin Craters actually consists of four separate vents aligned north-northeast.

28(C) Lost Woman Crater (right side of the photograph) from Cerro Rendija.

28(D) Lava Crater to the west, with its far wall partly in shadow in the center of the photograph.

Photographs courtesy of U.S. Geological Survey personnel.

Plate 29. *Fissure eruption of Kilauea Volcano, Hawaii, on the east rift zone in November 1979; note that the fissure is offset to the right in at least three places. Photograph courtesy of U.S. Geological Survey personnel.*

Plate 30. *A kipuka in the process of being formed as the active lava flows from Kilauea Volcano's east rift zone eruption of April 1983 surround an older spatter cone. Photograph courtesy of U.S. Geological Survey personnel.*

heat of a 10-foot-deep river of lava rushing through the tube. The floor is rough lava, the dregs that drained away through the tube as the flow died. The prominent gutters found about halfway along the tube also formed as the lava tube was dying. Near the back of the cave, the floor is rumpled, and then the cave is divided into two levels by a crust that cooled on the later lava. In this area of the cave, there are many delicate growths and crusts of white minerals that formed long after the lava tube cooled (Plate 26). Please avoid touching them or walking on sections of the cave floor where they are growing.

CATERPILLAR COLLAPSE

Following the trail beyond Four Windows Cave, the next feature to the north of the cave was named Caterpillar Collapse (Figure 15) because of its sinuous meanders. This long, winding section of trench was once a covered lava tube, whose roof has now completely collapsed. Much of this type of collapse occurs soon after a lava flow stops. As the red-hot walls of a lava tube cool, the rock contracts and weakens the roof of the tube. Still partly supported by the flowing lava underneath, the roof slowly sags, leaving the surface features largely intact. In the Caterpillar Collapse, the lava tube roof failed entirely. A roof can collapse slowly, sag, or collapse rapidly as at Seven Bridges Collapse.

SEVEN BRIDGES COLLAPSE

Located just south of Big Skylight Cave, this section of the tube system collapsed rapidly, leaving a steep-walled trench with a rubble floor. The rubble was once the roof of the lava tube. Seven natural bridges are the remains of the lava tube roof. The bridges were solid enough to withstand the pressure of rapidly collapsing rock on either side of the bridge. Follow the trail south of Big Skylight Cave

(Figure 15). The trail is less than ¼ mile and marked with rock cairns.

CERRO HOYA VOLCANO AND HOYA DE CIBOLA LAVA FLOW

Hu' Wa nani sha ste ka'nish (Keresan) Biih dahat`s o's (Navajo)

Cerro Hoya is a large shield volcano about 1.5 miles in diameter and 300 feet high located near the western edge of El Malpais National Monument (see Figure 5). In 1986, Charles Maxwell mapped Cerro Hoya and its flows as younger than the Twin Craters cluster of cones and flows. However, his map shows that the flows from Cerro Hoya and the Twin Craters group of vents are not in contact. They are separated at a key location by a flow from Bandera Crater. Since there is no radiocarbon date for Cerro Hoya, we do not know whether it or the Twin Craters group is younger.

Flows from Cerro Hoya traveled at least 33 miles from their vent, first to the southeast and then northeast. We estimate their volume to be as much as 1.8 cubic miles, depending on the unknown thicknesses of the flows. Lava tube systems in flows from Cerro Hoya are quite remarkable and include such features as Braided Cave.

BRAIDED CAVE

This exquisite cave, reached from County Road 42 (Figures 5 and 8) is accessible through several skylight collapses. Use monument maps to locate the parking area. It is about ¾ of a mile long. In addition to "bathtub rings" (Plate 22) and remelting features, a large block of sandstone approximately 3 feet long (Plate 27), now entirely remelted to pumice, lies on the tube floor near the cave's upper end. Another collapsed tube, at least 1.5 miles long, starts at a small vent about ⅝ mile north of Cerro Hoya.

CERRO CANDELARIA, TWIN CRATERS, LOST WOMAN CRATER, AND LAVA CRATER

These four cinder cones (Plates 28A, B, C, D) and their associated flows erupted at about the same time, around 16,000 years ago, according to Charles Maxwell (1986), A. W. Laughlin (1993), Tracey Cascadden (1997), and others. Because the abundance and size of olivine phenocrysts are about the same in basalts erupted by each cone, early workers had difficulty distinguishing relative ages of flows associated with each cone. However, recent work by Cascadden, who mapped the geology in considerable detail around the four cones and examined paleomagnetic secular variation in these flows, refined the sequence of eruptions. She found that Cerro Candelaria (private land) is the youngest vent, followed in order by Twin Craters, Lost Woman Crater, and Lava Crater (private land). Flows from these four vents traveled at least 16 miles east and northeast. We estimate the total volume of these eruptions to be about ¼ cubic mile. The two craters designated as being on private property are closed to the public. Despite such data research has been limited, and crucial facts concerning these prominent landmarks east of Bandera Crater remain unknown.

EL CALDERON VOLCANO AND ITS FLOWS

TSE MA SHA AA DAU SHI (KERESAN)
SHASH SIKÉHI (NAVAJO)

El Calderon is located 21 miles south of Interstate 40 along New Mexico 53 (Figures 5 and 8). Of the extensive, rugged lava flows that make up the present surface of El Malpais, El Calderon was the earliest to erupt (Figure 16). Older flows from vents in the Chain of Craters region undoubtedly underlie the young flows of El Malpais, but in most cases they are completely buried. Lava from El Calderon poured out about 115,000 to 120,000 years ago, according to Tracey

Figure 16. *El Calderon cinder cone from the southwest. Photograph courtesy of U.S. Geological Survey personnel.*

Cascadden and others (1997), during "Pulse 2" of A. W. Laughlin and others (1993). The eruption began as the ground cracked open to form fissures that sprayed lava near the site of the present cone, similar to the eruption of Kilauea Volcano pictured in Plate 29. A lava flow covered these vents, but the deposits from the fissures formed the low hills on the west and north sides of the cone. Lava began fountaining hundreds of feet in the air to form the cinder cone. Explosive blasts hurled bombs up to 3 feet in diameter over the rim of the crater. Molten lava falling back from the fire fountains made a river of lava that poured from the mouth of the crater. The river swept cinder away from the opening in the cone and fed the large flow that extends for several miles southeast of El Calderon.

As the fire fountains died, lava continued to well up and repeatedly overflowed the vent as very gas-rich, bubbly lava flows, building a lava shield on the northeast side of the cinder cone. Channels of slower-moving lava crusted over to form lava tubes that insulated the lava and allowed it to travel great distances. The low, partly soil-covered hills of lava west of the junction of Interstate 40 and New Mexico 117 came from the El Calderon shield. It probably took several years for these long lava flows to cover this large area. In 1997, Tracey Cascadden and others traced the El Calderon flow to about 2 miles east of the intersection of New Mexico 117 and Interstate 40, a distance of about 22 miles from the El Calderon cone. We estimate the volume of El Calderon flows to be at least 1 cubic mile.

As the tube system cooled, the roof collapsed, forming the extensive system of trenches and collapse pits on the shield above the present parking area. The thin shelly pahoehoe exposed in these collapses was formed by repeated overflows from the vent. Directly west of Bat Cave and upslope toward El Calderon is a shallow depression that was a small perched lava lake created by the damming of surface lava flows. This lake appears to be located at the beginning of the Bat Cave tube system (Figure 17), and the lake drained near the end of El Calderon's eruptions, through a lava tube which has two accessible caves today— Xenolith Cave (uphill or west of the trail) and Bat Cave, which is closed to the public to protect the bat colony.

The Double Sinks (Figure 17), the trail between Junction Cave and Bat Cave, are collapsed segments of another tube system in the El Calderon flows.

JUNCTION CAVE

Junction Cave (Figures 5 and 17) is a section of another complex tube system from the El Calderon shield volcano. This tube dives steeply off the shield, dropping over a 100 feet under the younger Lava Crater flow. Lava must have raced through this section of the tube, with a temperature so hot the walls melted and sagged, producing the rumply "elephant skin" texture. When the eruption stopped, most of the lava drained from the tube, leaving it hollow with an arched ceiling and a flat floor of sticky lava residue. Over the centuries blocks fell from the ceiling and now litter virtually all of the

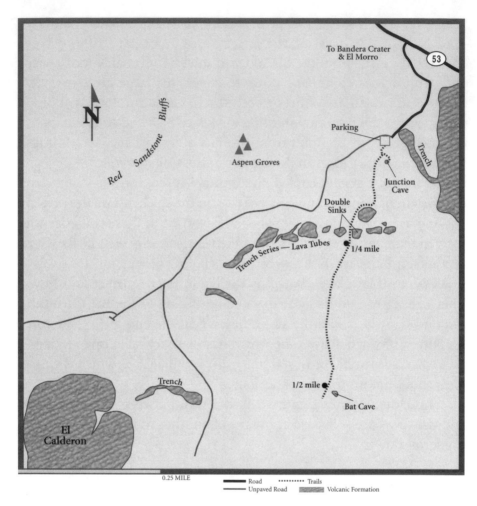

Figure 17. *Map showing Junction Cave area trail.*

cave. Because the opening of this cave is in the valley floor, it occasionally floods with muddy water as evidenced by the high watermarks midway up the cave walls. The far end of the cave is blocked by mud that is home to many cave insects. Please do not go past the closed signs.

All of the above features are included in a National Park Service hiking guide that is available at the head of the ½-mile trail.

FOR YOUR SAFETY

One of the oldest eruptive centers in the monument, the El Calderon area offers aboveground exploration of sinkholes, aspen groves, El Calderon Crater, and lava trenches, as well as underground exploration of Junction Cave, a 3,000-foot-long lava tube. For safety underground, take several light sources, wear sturdy boots, a hat, gloves, and protective clothing.

DIRECTIONS

Heading west on New Mexico 53, turn south soon after mile marker 66, approximately 20 miles from Interstate 40. The first ¼ mile is suitable for most vehicles. Other area roads require high clearance. Please stay on designated roads and take plenty of water with you. **Wet weather conditions can make these roads treacherous and impassable. Check with a ranger before you attempt to drive them. DO NOT TRAVEL ALONE.**

A Mexican free-tailed bat colony migrates between the caves in this area and Mexico. Flights can be observed at dusk during the summer from the knoll above the entrance to Bat Cave. Because of grave health risks to humans and disruption to the bats, do not go into any bat caves. If you are in a cave and come across bats, do not shine lights at or otherwise disturb them. These caves are their homes.

OTHER ZUÑI-BANDERA VOLCANIC FIELD LAVA FLOWS

As previously noted, cinder cones and lava flows of El Malpais National Monument are only part of the large Zuñi-Bandera volcanic field of northwestern New Mexico. Three other relatively young cones and their associated lava flows are located in the Zuñi Mountains a few miles north and northwest of Bandera Crater in the Cibola National Forest (Figure 5).

Figure 18. *Flow from Paxton Springs cone on the floor and walls of Zuñi Canyon. Photograph courtesy of U.S. Geological Survey personnel.*

PAXTON SPRINGS CONE AND ZUÑI CANYON FLOW

The cone near the historic settlement of Paxton Springs is about 4 miles north-northeast of Bandera Crater. From that source, one `a`a flow moved south about 2 miles, and another flowed northeast about 15 miles through Zuñi Canyon (Figure 18) to the vicinity of Grants. These flows overlie flows from both Oso Ridge and Cerro Colorado. Dating of the eruption indicates it occurred only a few tens of thousands of years ago. Refer to Figure 5 for access information to these sites. Additional information is available at the National Park Service Information Center on New Mexico 53.

Figure 19. *View to the southwest across El Malpais to the older cinder cones of the Chain of Craters. Photograph courtesy of U.S. Geological Survey personnel.*

CERRO COLORADO

A lava flow that originated at this cone, about 8 miles north of Paxton Springs, also flowed partway (at least 4 miles from the source) down Zuñi Canyon towards Grants, perhaps a few thousand years before the Paxton Springs eruption occurred. Charles Maxwell called this the "Zuñi flow." Refer to Figure 5 and the National Park Service brochure for information concerning roads and access.

OSO RIDGE CONE AND ITS FLOW

The cone and associated flow that cap Oso Ridge, about 3 miles northwest of Bandera Crater, are the oldest of the trio that erupted in

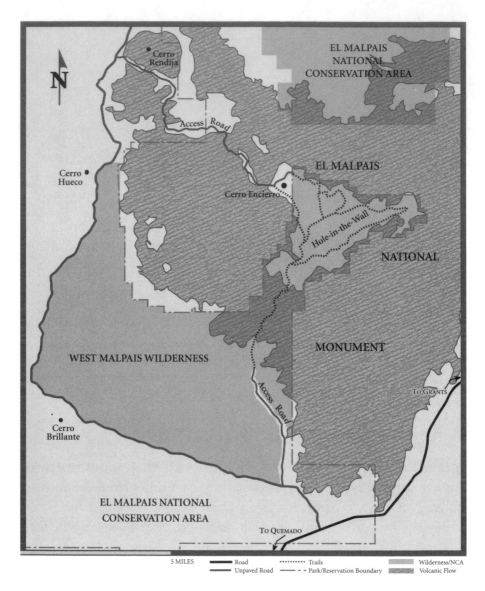

Figure 20. *Map of West Malpais Wilderness and Hole-in-the-Wall Trail.*

the Zuñi Mountains. The Oso Ridge flow moved about 6 miles east and southeast. In 1986, Charles Maxwell mapped the Oso Ridge flow as younger than the Cerro Candelaria-Twin Craters-Lost Woman

FOR YOUR SAFETY

Water is scarce in this arid region. You MUST carry with you all the water you will need. No mechanized vehicles may be driven past the posted wilderness boundary. **Wet weather conditions can make these roads treacherous and impassable. Check with a ranger before you attempt to drive them. DO NOT TRAVEL ALONE.** Obtain a back-country permit from El Malpais Information Center or the BLM El Malpais Ranger Station on New Mexico 117.

DIRECTIONS

The easiest way to access West Malpais Wilderness and Hole-in-the-Wall by car is from the south end of the El Malpais National Conservation Area off New Mexico 117. From New Mexico 117, proceed northwest on County Road 42 for about 2.1 miles. Take the right fork to the north and go approximately 5 miles up the "cherry stem" road to the West Malpais Wilderness trailhead.

Hole-in-the-Wall and the interior of West Malpais Wilderness can also be accessed from the north. Turn south from New Mexico 53 onto County Road 42 and proceed about 5.8 miles. Then turn left (east) on the road that skirts the south side of Cerro Rendija. (Warning: this is one of the roughest roads in the El Malpais National Conservation Area.) Continue on this road 2.1 miles, take the left fork, and go an additional .7 miles, then take the right fork. (The fork at this junction will take you to the Big Tubes area.) After another 1.2 miles, at the stock pond bear left again. In 1.5 miles you will see a sign for Hole-in-the-Wall. Continue straight for an additional .9 miles. At the single fence-post, bear right and continue straight on the main road for another 3.9 miles to the Cerro Encierro trailhead.

Crater-Lava Crater flows, although flows from the two centers are not in contact at the surface. The Paxton Springs, Cerro Colorado, and Oso Ridge eruptions all may have occurred less than 16,000 years ago. Refer to U.S. Geological Survey topographic maps and the National Park Service park brochure for access roads to these features.

CHAIN OF CRATERS AND
OLDER ERUPTIONS

El Malpais National Monument includes a few lava flows that are much older than the rough-surfaced lavas that give the monument its name. These cones (Figure 19) are best seen along the 33 miles of County Road 42. This dirt road runs along the west and south sides of the monument and links New Mexico 53 and 117. Check on road conditions before traveling on this route as it is treacherous when wet. Some of the more notable of these older eruptive centers, known as the Chain of Craters, are Cerro Bandera (private land); Cerro Rendija, a large shield volcano 2 miles in diameter and 500 feet high with several lava tubes; Cerro Arizona, dated at about 150,000 years B.P. according to A. W. Laughlin and others (1993); Cerro Hueco; Cerro Brillante; Cerro Encierro (on the northwestern edge of Hole-in-the-Wall (Figure 20), a large 12-square-mile kipuka, or island of older lava (Plate 30); and Cerro Americano, which is almost perfectly circular and composed of bright red and yellow cinders.

The foreboding beauty of El Malpais is distinctive when compared to other volcanic areas of the world. As Alton Lindsey, the premier researcher of the area in the early 1940s, observed in the introduction to the 1997 book *The Natural History of El Malpais National Monument:* "Today's monument is a living laboratory for the uniqueness of the area." Here visitors and scientists can hike across lava formations and forested cinder cones, look into a crater at ancient lava bombs that blasted the surface, study unusual basalt tree molds, walk among slow-growing, very long-lived pygmy tree forests on the rugged lava surface of an `a`a field, or gaze into sunken gardens at moisture-loving spleenwort ferns. They can even explore ice caves, where rare algae previously only found in Antarctica thrive, or see what Lindsey called "goblin gold," an incandescent, microscopic alga unknown anywhere else in the world. El Malpais remains an astonishing opus to nature's creative evolution. The importance of this lava masterpiece has been made clear during the thirty-seven years of research and scientific discovery that has proved there is always something more to be learned from this black rock.

8

FUTURE ERUPTIONS
AT EL MALPAIS

I t is interesting to attempt to determine when El Malpais might
erupt again. The estimated 100 eruptions during the past million
years at El Malpais indicate that the average interval between
eruptions was about 10,000 years. On that basis, and considering the
McCartys Crater erupted about 3,000 years ago, future eruptions
might not occur for another 7,000 years. From another perspective,
about 8,000 years elapsed between the Bandera Crater and McCartys
eruptions, and only 5,000 years between the group of eruptions at
Cerro Candelaria/Twin Craters/Lost Woman Crater/Lava Crater and
the Bandera Crater event. Thus, perhaps 5,000 to 8,000 years is a rea-
sonable estimate of the average interval between eruptions during the
last few 10,000 years.

To refine our understanding of the volcanic history of the area,
we are currently collecting charcoal to date more of the young eruptions at El Malpais, such as those of Cerro Hoya. In addition, our
research of other volcanoes has added to our knowledge of eruptive
patterns. For example, we have learned that eruptions occur in clus-
ters rather than evenly spaced in time. However, despite such
research and speculation, ultimately we do not know when any

future eruptions might occur at El Malpais. What we do know is that there will be plenty of warning, because many small volcanic earthquakes, indicating the cracking of rock as magma ascends, will rattle the region prior to any eruption. In the meantime, both visitors and scientists can continue to appreciate and acquire important knowledge from the area's many fascinating formations.

GLOSSARY

`a`a lava flow. A Hawaiian term for a lava flow that mainly consists of rubble or clinker and is often very sharp. The top and bottom of an `a`a flow often consist of loose clinker, separated by a central massive layer that represents the solidified, formerly molten core. Cross-sectional exposures showing these features are often seen in road cuts around El Malpais National Monument (see Plate 18).

`a`a sheet flow. An `a`a flow that advances without benefit of lava channels or heat-conserving lava tubes and has a rough surface (see Plate 19).

agglutinate. Spatter or cinders that fall back to the ground while still molten. In partly agglutinated rock, the individual fragments can be seen but are welded together so they are no longer loose. Completely agglutinated rocks contain only ghosts of the original particles and look like very dense lava flows with very few vesicles. Dense layers of this type can be seen on the west and north walls of Bandera Crater (see Figure 6).

basalt. The most abundant lava on the earth, basalt is usually black when fresh, brown when old and weathered, and red where locally oxidized. It consists mainly of plagioclase feldspar (one of the most common minerals on the earth) and pyroxene (a silicate mineral of calcium, magnesium, and iron). Basalt also usually contains olivine, magnetite (an iron oxide), and lesser amounts of other minerals. Basalt most commonly occurs as `a`a or pahoehoe flows and as thin blades called dikes, or sills, on older rocks. All of the lavas at El Malpais are basalts.

bomb. Rounded lava that has been thrown through the air by a volcano. Bombs can range in size from 1 inch to more than 3 feet in diameter. They may have dense cores, but many bombs are full of vesicles. Names for many different types of volcanic bombs are based on their shapes, such as ribbon bomb, bread crust bomb, and cowpie bomb. Bombs that were partly molten when they fell, and thus had long tails and aerodynamic bodies, are called spindle bombs; nearly spherical bombs, which were solidified before they were blown out of the crater, are called accretionary bombs. Good examples are on display at the visitor centers (see Figures 4A and 4B).

breached cone. A cone whose symmetry has been broken by a lava flow that interrupts the smooth continuity of the crater rim. Bandera Crater is the most accessible example. In Plate 12, the breach is on the left side of the cone.

cinder. A fragment of lava that has been vigorously ejected from a volcano. Often somewhat rounded and nearly equidimensional, cinders range in size from about ⅛ inch to 3 inches or more and usually are full of vesicles. Cinders can be seen at all cones in the monument (see Plates 9 and 10).

cinder cone. A hill that forms by the accumulation of cinders around a volcanic vent. Cinder cones range in height from a few tens of feet to 1,500 feet or more, and in diameter from as little as 100 feet to over a mile. Cinders and spatter are often erupted during different episodes in the building of a cone, and the resulting feature may be called a cinder-and-spatter cone (see Plate 12).

crater (volcanic). A depression, often more or less circular, in a volcanic cone or flow. Craters may form in many different ways. Craters in cones result from the accumulation of cinders, lava, or spatter around a vent, or from the withdrawal of near-surface magma and subsequent collapse of part of the cone. Other craters form when lava piles up around the edge of a preexisting high area that then becomes relatively low (see Plate 11).

curtain of fire. A line of adjacent lava fountains along an eruptive fissure, sometimes extending discontinuously for a distance of several miles. Curtains of fire are typical features at the beginning of an eruption of Hawaiian volcanoes (see Plate 3).

dacite. Lava rich in silica (about ⅔ window glass).

dripstone. A general term for any cave feature formed by dripping water or lava; in this guidebook, it refers mainly to lava stalactites, stalagmites, and similar features in lava tubes. Good examples can be seen in Big Skylight Cave, Four Windows Cave, and Braided Cave (see Plates 21 and 25).

feldspar. A group of minerals mainly composed of the elements silicon and aluminum, with variable proportions of calcium, sodium, and potassium. Feldspars are the most common minerals in the earth's crust, and plagioclase feldspar is the most abundant mineral in basalt. Feldspars are generally white or pink; some plagioclase phenocrysts in El Malpais basalts are colorless, clear, and almost glassy.

fire fountain. Eruption of incandescent spatter or cinders from a central volcanic vent or fissure system, characterized by minor fluctuations in column height and duration (see Plate 4).

fissure eruption. Eruption of lava, as spatter, cinders, and flows from an elongated surface crack. Fissure eruptions in Hawaii and elsewhere typically start with a curtain of fire that may extend discontinuously for several miles. Eruptions usually eventually become concentrated at a single vent or small group of closely spaced vents. This type of eruption may have occurred along the east side of the McCartys flow (see Plates 5 and 29).

granite. A plutonic igneous rock, meaning that it was once molten and solidified underground, in contrast to a volcanic rock. Granite is the chemical equivalent of rhyolite and is the silica-rich end product of igneous rock chemical compositions. Granites generally consist of large, easily visible crystals of quartz, feldspar, and mica. The crystals are large because they had more time to grow, being insulated from relatively cold air at the earth's surface.

hornito. (Spanish for "little oven") A small spatter cone built over a crack on an active lava flow. Hornitoes generally range from about 5 to 30 feet high and are often called rootless because they are not directly connected to the subterranean magma reservoir that feeds the eruptive vent (see Figure 9).

hummocky pahoehoe. A pahoehoe lava that has blisters or tumuli
on its surface. Examples can be seen along the Lava Falls Trail.

igneous. Pertaining to a rock or mineral that solidified from magma.

inflated pahoehoe. A pahoehoe lava flow whose thickness has been
greatly increased since it first erupted because of sustained input
of new lava during a long-lived eruption (see Plates 23 A and B).

inflation depression. A depression that forms as lava cools where
there was less gas trapped in the molten rock than the surrounding terrain, or where a thinner layer of lava flows over the land
(see also "inflation ridge").

inflation ridge. A ridge that forms as lava cools and the trapped
gasses inflate the rock higher than the surrounding terrain. The
inflation process is very similar to the way shaving cream expands
when it comes out of the can (see also "inflation depression").

kipuka. A Hawaiian word meaning "island" of older lava (or other
rock) surrounded by younger lava flows. Kipukas often have special
botanical importance because they contain older soils and more
mature ecosystems. At El Malpais, features named "Hole-in-the-
Wall" and "Little Hole-in-the- Wall" are large kipukas (see Plate 30).

lava. Molten rock flowing on the earth's surface.

lava blister. A lava formation that occurs as a result of gas in the flow
expanding and inflating the pahoehoe surface (see also "inflation
ridge").

lava flow. An outpouring of molten rock from a volcanic vent onto
the earth's surface. Also the solidified stream or sheet of rock
formed in this manner (see also "magma" and Plate 15).

lava lake. A lake of fluid molten lava, ordinarily contained in a summit crater or a pit crater on the side of a shield volcano. Once the
molten lava drains, the resulting depression is called a "perched
lava lake."

lava tube. A cave within a lava flow formed by the complete or par-
tial withdrawal of molten lava after formation of the surface
crust. The term is used both when the lava flow is active and
when it has solidified. El Malpais has at least five major systems of

lava tubes. The best-known caves include Junction Cave, Big Skylight Cave, Four Windows Cave, and Braided Cave.

lava tumulus. A lava formation larger than a blister that forms on gentle slopes when the flow's advance is obstructed and lava beneath the surface inflates the crust. These are common features found throughout the monument (see Figure 12A).

magma. Molten rock that is stored within the earth or traveling to the eruption site. Once the molten material erupts at the surface it is called lava.

magma chamber. A reservoir of magma beneath a volcano before eruption. Magma chambers usually are within a few hundreds of feet to several miles below the earth's surface.

mantle. The region of the earth between the crust (the part we live on) and the core. The crust that forms the continents is typically 20 to 30 miles thick, while ocean crust is only about 10 miles thick. Most of the earth's interior is the mantle, which is primarily composed of the mineral olivine, the green mineral found in most of the lava flows at El Malpais. Basalt magma is produced when a small amount of the mantle melts and rises into the crust.

mineral. A naturally formed chemical element, or compound of two or more elements, having a characteristic crystal form. Some common, well-known minerals include quartz, feldspar, olivine, and mica.

monogenetic. A cinder cone and associated flows that formed during a single eruption.

olivine. A light green mineral typically found in basaltic lavas such as those of El Malpais. It is a compound of silicon, iron, and magnesium. Rocks made up mostly of olivine are called peridotites, after peridot, the gem-quality olivine.

pahoehoe lava flow. A Hawaiian term for relatively smooth-surfaced lava, often displaying ropy texture. Long-lived pahoehoe flows typically advance when lava flows in tubes, which conserve heat and retard chilling and solidification. This type of flow is common throughout the monument (see Plate 17).

pahoehoe sheet flow. A pahoehoe flow that lacks surface channels or underground tubes and has a relatively smooth upper surface, characteristically emplaced on nearly horizontal preexisting surfaces. This type of flow is best seen on the east side of the monument from Sandstone Bluffs (see Plate 16).

peridotite. A rock that consists mainly of olivine, with lesser amounts of pyroxene and spinal (see Plate 6).

phenocryst. A large mineral crystal, visible with the naked eye, surrounded by smaller, often microscopic, crystals or glass. A rock that contains phenocrysts is called a "porphyry." Olivine and plagioclase are the most common phenocryst minerals in the basalts of El Malpais.

plagioclase. A feldspar mineral consisting of silicon and aluminum with variable amounts of sodium and calcium. Plagioclase, usually pink in color, is a major constituent of basalt.

pyroclastic. Pertaining to rock material thrown through the air by a volcanic explosion.

pyroxene. A dark green, black, or brown mineral typically found in basaltic lavas such as those of El Malpais. Pyroxene is a compound of silicon, iron, magnesium, and calcium.

rhyolite. Lava rich in silica (about ¾ window glass).

shelly pahoehoe. Pahoehoe so thin, light, and full of gas holes that it breaks like a shell when stepped on.

shield volcano. A relatively low, gently-sloped volcano, a few hundred yards to several tens of miles in diameter, constructed mainly of lava flows with little pyroclastic material. The resulting profile is shaped like a shield, pointing skyward. Cerro Hoya and Cerro Rendija are examples of shield volcanoes in El Malpais National Monument (see Plate 14).

silica. A compound of the elements silicon and oxygen (SiO_2), more commonly called quartz.

skylight. An opening into a lava tube. Skylights may open during the flow event, as seen at Big Skylight Cave, or after the flow has become inactive, as seen at Four Windows Cave.

slab pahoehoe. A lava flow that is transitional between pahoehoe and `a`a lava. A pahoehoe flow whose surface has been broken into slabs, often several feet or more across but generally only a few inches thick. An accumulation of slabs may result from withdrawal of support from beneath the crust, from lateral pressure induced by another flow lobe, or by lava cascading over a small incline. Slab pahoehoe can be, but is not always, an intermediate stage between initial pahoehoe and later `a`a. This is a common feature at El Malpais National Monument.

spatter. Very fluid lava ejected from a volcano, characteristically forming flattened or ribbon-shaped bombs. Fragments of spatter can range in size from less than 1 inch to several feet long. If enough spatter accumulates in one place over a short time, its heat causes the fragments to weld together, obscuring the original pyroclastic structure and forming agglutinate or agglutinated spatter (see also "spatter cone," below, and Plate 8).

spatter cone. A steep-sided cone of spatter built around a volcanic vent. Spatter cones can range from a few feet to hundreds of feet high and can be 1 mile or more in diameter. Examples can be seen on the trails at Bandera Crater (private), near the Big Tubes Trail, or in the backcountry (see Plate 7).

spinel. A black, brown, or green oxide mineral that is a compound of magnesium, aluminum, iron, chromium, and other metals. Spinel is often found in xenoliths that have been brought up from the earth's mantle by magma. Magnetite, common in basalts of El Malpais, is a member of the spinel family of minerals.

spiny pahoehoe. A lava flow whose surface texture is transitional between pahoehoe and `a`a; characteristically it has abundant knobby protuberances of lava a few inches in diameter and height.

stratovolcano. A large volcano composed of alternating layers of pyroclastic and flow material. Commonly used synonyms are "composite volcano" or "composite cone." Stratovolcanoes may reach several miles above their bases and be several miles in diameter. Some of the most beautiful, symmetrical volcanoes in the world are stratovolcanoes, such as Mount Fuji in Japan and the pre-1980 Mount St. Helens in Washington State. Mount Taylor, north of Grants (see Figure 2 and Plate 2) is this type of volcano.

tube-fed pahoehoe. Pahoehoe that has flowed through lava tubes.

vesicle. A rounded cavity of variable shape in a volcanic rock, formed by the entrapment of a gas bubble during solidification (see Plate 20).

xenolith. From the Greek meaning "foreign rock." An inclusion of an older, different rock in an igneous rock, such as basalt. A mantle xenolith originally was a piece of solid or nearly solid rock in the earth's mantle, recognized as such by having constituent minerals that formed under higher pressure than exists in the shallower crust of the earth. Mantle xenoliths, common in basaltic cinder cones and lava flows in many places on the earth's surface, can be seen at El Malpais in the Bandera flows (see Plates 6 and 27).

ENGLISH-METRIC CONVERSIONS

1 mile=1.61 kilometers
1 cubic mile=4.17 cubic kilometers
0.04 inch=0.001 millimeter
1 inch=0.39 centimeters
1 foot=30.5 centimeters
1 foot=0.305 meters

BIBLIOGRAPHY

Carden, J. R., and A. W. Laughlin. "Petrochemical Variations within the McCartys Basalt Flow, Valencia County, New Mexico." *Geological Society of America Bulletin* 85 (1974): 1479, 1484.

Cascadden, T. E., J. W. Geissman, and A. M. Kudo. "Short-lived Eruption of Heterogeneous Magma in the Central Zuñi-Bandera Volcanic Field (Cerro Candelaria, Twin Craters, Lost Woman Crater, and La Tetera): Paleomagnetism and Geochemical Data." *New Mexico Bureau of Mines and Mineral Resources Bulletin* (1997).

Cascadden, T. E., J. W. Geissman, A. M. Kudo, and A. W. Laughlin. "El Calderon Cinder Cone and Related Basalt Flows." *New Mexico Bureau of Mines and Mineral Resources Bulletin* (1998).

Decker, R. W., T. L. Wright, and P. H. Stauffer, eds. *Volcanism in Hawaii:U.S. Geological Survey Professional Paper* 1350 (1987).

Fisher, R.V., and H. U. Schmincke. *Pyroclastic Rocks.* Berlin: Springer-Verlag, 1984.

Green, Jack, and N. M. Short. *Volcanic Land Forms and Surface Features: A Photographic Atlas and Glossary.* New York: Springer-Verlag, 1971.

Hon, Ken, Jim Kauahikaua, Roger Denlinger, and Kevin Mackay. "Emplacement and Inflation of Pahoehoe Sheet Flows: Observations and Measurements of Active Lava Flows on Kilauea Volcano, Hawaii." *Geological Society of America Bulletin* 106 (1994): 351–70.

Laughlin, A. W., R. W. Charles, Kevin Reid, and Carol White. "Field-trip Guide to the Geochronology of El Malpais National Monument and the Zuñi-Bandera Volcanic Field, New Mexico." *New Mexico Bureau of Mines and Mineral Resources Bulletin* 149 (1993).

Mabery, Ken, comp. "Natural History of El Malpais National Monument." *New Mexico Bureau of Mines and Mineral Resources Bulletin* 156 (1997).

Mabery, Marilyne V. *El Malpais National Monument.* Tucson, Ariz.: Southwest Parks and Monuments Association, 1989.

_____. *Web of Culture: A Thousand-Year Cultural History of El Malpais.* Ann Arbor, Mich.: UMI Company, 1998.

Maxwell, Charles H. "Geologic Map of El Malpais Lava Field and Surrounding Areas, Cibola County, New Mexico." *U.S. Geological Survey Miscellaneous Investigations Series Map* I-1595.

Nichols, R. L. "McCartys Basalt Flow, Valencia County, New Mexico." *Geological Society of America Bulletin* 57, no. 11 (1946): 1049–086.

Slifer, Dennis. *Signs of Life: Rock Art of the Upper Rio Grande.* Santa Fe, N.M.: Ancient City Press, 1998.

USGS. *Dictionary of Geological Terms.* Garden City, N.Y.: Doubleday& Company, 1997

INDEX